The GREATEST MOMENTS in SPORTS

UPSETS

AND

UNDERDOGS

LEN BERMAN

sourcebooks
jabberwocky

For Eli:

Dream large.

Len Berman was recorded by Pomann Sound, New York, New York.

Some audio segments have been edited for time and content. Some archival audio quality is the result of source limitations. Archival audio copyright and used with permission of:

CBS Sports, Inc.	Major League Baseball Properties, Inc.	NBC Sports, Inc.
HBO Sports, Inc.	NASCAR, Inc.	XOS Technologies, Inc.

All efforts have been made by the editors to contact the copyright holders for the material used in this book. The editors regret any omissions that may have occurred and will correct any such errors in future printings of this book.

Special thanks to the amazing broadcasters who brought to life the great moments on our CD:

Dick Bank	Russ Hodges	Larry Merchant
Sandra Bezic	Mike Joy	Bud Palmer
Jeff Blatnick	Jim Lampley	Ara Parseghian
Tim Daggett	Sugar Ray Leonard	John Tesh
Pat Haden	Sean McDonough	Elfi Schlegel
Scott Hamilton	Larry McReynolds	Darrell Waltrip
Tom Hammond	Matt Millen	
Russ Hellickson	Brent Musburger	

Published by Sourcebooks Jabberwocky, an imprint of Sourcebooks, Inc.
P.O. Box 4410, Naperville, Illinois 60567-4410
(630) 961-3900
Fax: (630) 961-2168
www.jabberwockykids.com

Library of Congress Cataloging-in-Publication data is on file with the publisher.

Source of Production: LeHigh, Hagerstown, Maryland, USA
Date of Production: August 2012
Run Number: 18262

Printed and bound in the United States of America.
LEH 10 9 8 7 6 5 4 3 2 1

CONTENTS

INTRODUCTION

In sports, everybody roots for the underdog. They want to see the athlete or the team with no chance overcome long odds to emerge victorious. This isn't something new. It goes back thousands of years. It's right there in the Bible. Was the first upset David versus Goliath? It might have been. A small boy with a slingshot slew a mighty giant. And now, all these centuries later, when an underdog takes the field against a mighty opponent, it's still referred to as David versus Goliath.

That's what this book is all about—the little guy, the underdog, the team with no shot pulling a major upset against all odds. In fact, one story is about a horse named Upset. Upset pulled off one of the greatest upsets in horse-racing history—so great that some people mistakenly think his name is where the term *upset* comes from.

If the underdogs are not Davids, they might be Cinderellas. You know the story. Cinderella is treated poorly by her wicked stepmother and stepsisters. Thanks to her fairy godmother, she winds up at a beautiful ball but has to get home before midnight, when the spell will be broken. Stories of sports teams that far exceed expectations are often referred to as Cinderella stories. Their fans hope they can become champions before midnight strikes and the magic wears off.

In the following pages, you will read story after story of Davids and Cinderellas. Many of them read like fairy tales. And that's the best part about these events. They are not made-up Hollywood movies, although some of these stories served as the source of inspiration for great sports films. They are all true amazing stories of upsets and underdogs.

How amazing? Several of them are described using the word *miracle*. There's the "Miracle on Ice," the "Miracle of Coogan's Bluff," the "Miracle Mets"—and that's just for starters. Yup, many of these upsets are considered miraculous.

Maybe you feel like an underdog—either in sports or otherwise. Perhaps you think you won't be able to succeed. Well, don't give up. After reading this book, you just might believe that anything is possible.

And if you find yourself rooting for the underdog, you are not alone. Everyone does.

I'd love to know which is your favorite chapter. You can email me at www.ThatsSports.com and let me know why. I look forward to hearing from you.

Len Berman

UPSET

So why is an unexpected sports result called an upset? We don't know for sure, but some people think it's because of a horse race way back in 1919. The greatest racehorse at the time was named Man o' War, and one day in upstate New York, he was upset by a less successful horse. That horse's name? Upset. Honest. And it was considered a huge upset. Many people think that because of that race, the word *upset* worked its way into common usage in the English language. That may or may not be true, but it serves to reinforce why Upset's win was one of the most surprising results in the history of sports.

MAN O' WAR

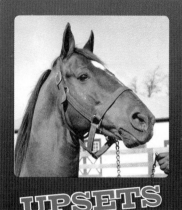

UPSETS AND UNDERDOGS

BORN: March 29, 1917

BIRTHPLACE: Lexington, KY

HEIGHT: 16.2 hands

WEIGHT: 1,125 lbs.

WINS: 20

LOSSES: 1

ROOKIE YEAR: 1919

NICKNAME: Big Red

CAREER HIGHLIGHTS: Considered one of the best racehorses of all time; won $249,465 in prize money; inducted into the National Museum of Racing and Hall of Fame in 1957.

Man o' War was much bigger than other racehorses of his time. That's probably because he ate **12 QUARTS OF OATS EVERY DAY**— about three quarts more than most horses!

Man o' War was born on March 29, 1917, near Lexington, Kentucky. His owner was August Belmont Jr., the builder of Belmont Park, a famous racetrack in New York. One of the biggest races in the world, the Belmont Stakes, bears his name. It was wartime when Man o' War was born, and that's how he got his name. August Belmont went off to France to fight in World War I; his wife was going to name the horse "My Man o' War," but the "My" somehow got dropped. While overseas, Mr. Belmont decided to sell all his racehorses, and Man o' War was sold for just $5,000 to a man named Samuel Riddle. From such humble beginnings, the legend of Man o' War grew.

He was a big horse with a big appetite. His color was chestnut, which is in the red family, so he picked up the nickname "Big Red." He raced 21 times in his short two-year career. He wasn't entered in the Kentucky Derby, but he did run the Preakness and the Belmont Stakes, winning both of those Triple Crown races.

To show you how great Man o' War became, he ran out of horses to race against. The other owners didn't want to compete with Man o' War because they were convinced they would lose. In 1920 only one horse dared to face him in the Belmont Stakes, which Man o' War easily won by a whopping 20 lengths.

In another race at Belmont Park called the Lawrence Realization Stakes, his only opponent was a horse named Hoodwink. Man o' War not only beat Hoodwink, but he trounced him by an amazing 100 lengths! Along the way, Man o' War set a world record for the distance of

1⅝ miles. The legend of Man o' War was growing larger and larger. He was compared with Babe Ruth as one of the biggest sports personalities of the 1920s. His career earnings were about $250,000, which was a great deal of money back then.

Man o' War finished racing in 1920. Talk about going out in style. He raced 11 times that year and won every single race. He was the obvious winner of Horse of the Year honors. He then retired to stud, where horse owners tried to breed more great racehorses from him. Man o' War was quite successful as a dad. He fathered horses that won 64 stakes races. One of those horses was War Admiral, who went on to

FAST FACT

Another great champion, Secretariat, was also known by the nickname "Big Red," but experts agree that Man o' War was the original.

win the Triple Crown in 1937. Wow—what a horse, Man o' War!

Then there was Upset. If it weren't for what happened on August 13, 1919, nobody would remember him. Upset was owned by a famous horseman named Harry Payne Whitney. During Upset's three-year career, he raced 17 times. He won five of those races and finished second seven times. Not bad. His career earnings were a mere $37,000. Upset nearly won the 1920 Kentucky Derby. He finished second—just a head behind the winner, Paul Jones.

By August 1919, Man o' War was starting to make a name for himself as a two-year-old. He had raced six times and won them all. On August 13, he was entered to run in the Sanford Stakes in Saratoga Springs, New York. And that's where he met up

HE WAS BRED IN OLD KENTUCKY

107445

The legendary race horse Man o' War won 21 out of 22 starts.

Upset holds off Man o' War to win the 1919 Stanford Stakes at Saratoga. This was the only time Man o' War finished out of first place.

Even though Man o' War beat Upset in six other races, everyone remembers this matchup the best.

with Upset. At the time, it wasn't considered to be a big deal. The two horses had faced each other just 11 days earlier on the same track, and Man o' War had come out the winner. The main competition for Man o' War was supposed to be a horse named Golden Broom.

But what happened on August 13 is not only legendary but it was controversial as well. In those days, horses didn't have a starting gate to begin the race. So basically, a piece of tape was strung across the track, and all the horses would line up behind it. Then the race starter would pull the tape, and the horses would be sent on their merry way. Well, according to the National Museum of Racing and Hall of Fame, the regular race starter wasn't on hand that day. His substitute was a man named Charles H. Pettingill. He was a man in his

70s who had problems with his eyesight. Man o' War was always anxious to race, and he would often break through the tape early, forcing the race to be restarted. That fateful day, he broke through five times, and every time, the race had to be stopped. On the sixth try, Man o' War wasn't quite ready to go. In fact, he was turned sideways when Pettingill started the race.

Johnny Loftus was Man o' War's jockey, and he had a lot of terrain to make up. There were seven horses in the race, and early on, Loftus and Man o' War were stuck in fifth place. Loftus was patient, waiting for the right moment to make his move. He kept gaining ground, and finally, there were just two horses in front of him—Golden Broom and Upset. Loftus wanted to take Man o' War to the inside, but he was boxed out by both horses. His only chance was to go to the outside. He was able to pass Golden Broom and now only Upset was between Man o' War and the finish line.

Willie Knapp was the jockey aboard Upset. Here's how he described the next frantic moments of the race. "I heard something right behind me and I knew it was Big Red coming at me now. I looked back and there he was. Johnny Loftus was riding like a crazy man and he yelled at me, 'Move out, Willie! I'm coming through!' So I yelled back at him, 'Take off! Take off me, bum, or I'll put you through the rail!' Then I set down to riding and we won."

Man o' War didn't like wearing riding gear at first. But a smart stable hand realized that if you asked Man o' War for permission, he would be OK with it.

Willie Knapp and Upset won indeed—by a mere half a length. Most observers felt that if the race were a little longer, Man o' War would have caught up to Upset and passed him. But it was not to be.

Stable employees said that Man o' War had nightmares for weeks after his loss. When he retired, Man o' War had raced 21 times and only lost that once. He set three world records, two American records, and a couple of track records. His jockey, Johnny Loftus, was elected to the Hall of Fame, as was Upset's jockey, Willie Knapp.

As for Man o' War and Upset, they wound up facing each other seven times. Man o' War won the other six races. And when they listed the top 100 U.S. Thoroughbred champions of the 20th century, guess who topped the list? Man o' War was voted number one. In any language, he would have been a perfect champion but for one blemish: an upset by Upset.

HOOSIERS

Bobby Plump of Milan keeps the ball from Willie Mason of Crispus Attucks in the semifinal game.

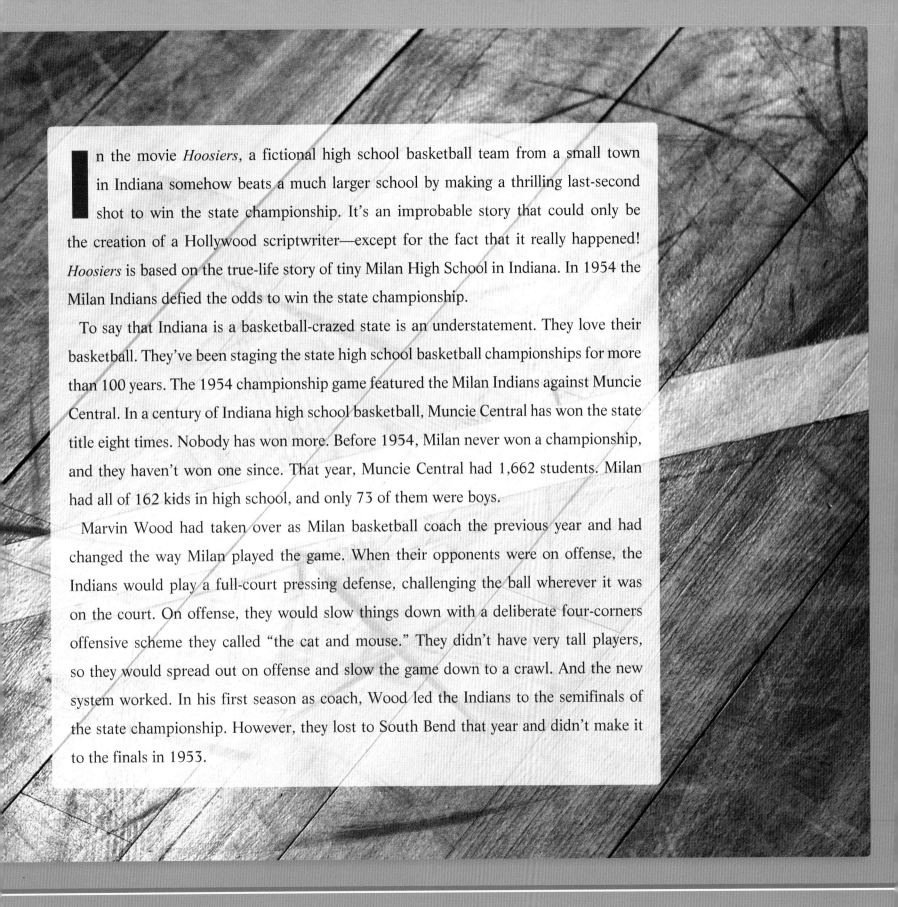

In the movie *Hoosiers*, a fictional high school basketball team from a small town in Indiana somehow beats a much larger school by making a thrilling last-second shot to win the state championship. It's an improbable story that could only be the creation of a Hollywood scriptwriter—except for the fact that it really happened! *Hoosiers* is based on the true-life story of tiny Milan High School in Indiana. In 1954 the Milan Indians defied the odds to win the state championship.

To say that Indiana is a basketball-crazed state is an understatement. They love their basketball. They've been staging the state high school basketball championships for more than 100 years. The 1954 championship game featured the Milan Indians against Muncie Central. In a century of Indiana high school basketball, Muncie Central has won the state title eight times. Nobody has won more. Before 1954, Milan never won a championship, and they haven't won one since. That year, Muncie Central had 1,662 students. Milan had all of 162 kids in high school, and only 73 of them were boys.

Marvin Wood had taken over as Milan basketball coach the previous year and had changed the way Milan played the game. When their opponents were on offense, the Indians would play a full-court pressing defense, challenging the ball wherever it was on the court. On offense, they would slow things down with a deliberate four-corners offensive scheme they called "the cat and mouse." They didn't have very tall players, so they would spread out on offense and slow the game down to a crawl. And the new system worked. In his first season as coach, Wood led the Indians to the semifinals of the state championship. However, they lost to South Bend that year and didn't make it to the finals in 1953.

In the movie, the coach of fictional Hickory High School measured the height of the basket at Butler Fieldhouse with the whole team watching. He wants to prove that despite playing in a huge arena, the baskets are the same size as the ones in the team's tiny home gym. It is a memorable scene, and it proves a great point—but it never happened. Hollywood made it up.

Actor Gene Hackman plays the coach of a small town basketball team in a scene from the movie *Hoosiers*, inspired by Milan's state championship win.

As Coach Marvin Wood would say, it's not like Milan snuck up on anybody in 1954. After their success the previous year and with most of the team returning, the Indians had a terrific regular season. They lost only two games, entering the postseason tournament with a 19–2 record.

The Indiana state championship is a virtual season unto itself. In 1954 there were 751 high schools in the tournament. For a team to win the state title, it has to survive a long grind of sectional and regional games before getting to the state semifinals. When all is said and done, the eventual champion has to play nine extra games and win them all!

First up were the sectionals in Versailles, Indiana. The Indians cruised in their first game, easily beating Cross Plains, 83–36. Then it was a 12-point victory over Osgood and a 14-point win over hometown Versailles. Three games, three wins. Next up, the regionals in Rushville.

Once again, the Indians had to play the host team, and they dispatched Rushville, 58–34. Then came the first real test: Aurora. That was one of the two teams that had beaten them in the regular season—but they couldn't do it again. An eight-point Milan win, and it was on to the semistate at Butler Fieldhouse. Two more wins, and the Indians would earn a return trip to the final four.

Their first opponent was Montezuma, a school even smaller than Milan. The Indians won by 10. Next up, Crispus Attucks. Although Milan didn't have any big stars, Crispus Attucks was led by Oscar Robertson, who went on to become one of the greatest players in college and NBA history—a basketball Hall of Famer. He led Crispus Attucks to championships in 1955 and 1956 but not in 1954. Milan won the game 65–52. Now the unlikely Milan Indians needed just two more wins and they would be the state champs.

The final four was played at Butler University's fieldhouse in Indianapolis, now known as Hinkle Fieldhouse. That was where *Hoosiers* was filmed. First up, the semifinal game in the afternoon—the game that Milan had lost the previous year. Not this time. Milan dispatched Terre Haute, 60–48. Milan had arrived! They would now face powerhouse Muncie Central that

Bobby Plump almost fifty years later poses with his championship jacket and his childhood hoop.

1954 MILAN STATE CHAMPIONSHIP TEAM

Coach Marvin Wood	Bill Jordan
Team Manager Fred Busching	Bobby Plump
	Roger Schroder
Glenn Butte	Ron Truitt
Ray Craft	Ken Wendelman
Rollin Cutter	Gene White
Bob Engel	Bob Wichman

night for the Indiana state championship. Milan had never played in a final, while the Bearcats had appeared in seven championship games and won four times, including 1951 and 1952. Needless to say, Muncie was the overwhelming favorite to win its fifth state title.

The date was March 20, 1954, a cold, snowy night outside. Inside, what would later become known as the "Milan Miracle" was about to take place. Milan played its typically tough defense and slow "cat and mouse" offense. After three quarters, the low-scoring game was tied 26–26.

There was no shot clock in operation, so Milan's Bobby Plump would stand for long periods of time just holding the ball without moving. It was perfectly legal. In fact, in the entire fourth quarter, there were only three baskets made by both teams combined, plus some foul shots.

With 1:43 left in the game, Plump made two free throws to give Milan a 30–28 lead. Then the Indians forced a turnover and got the ball back. Suddenly, Ray Craft drove for the basket, and he got open for an easy layup. But the ball hung on the rim for a second and fell off—no good. With one minute left, Muncie had the ball and a chance to tie the game. Gene Flowers didn't disappoint. The Bearcats leading scorer drove and tied the game at 30 with just 45 seconds remaining. With 18 seconds left, Milan called a timeout. Everyone in the fieldhouse knew who would try to take the winning shot: Bobby Plump. He was the team's high scorer in the tournament. Sure enough, Plump had the ball with the final seconds ticking away. *Ten, nine, eight, seven, six...*and then he made his move. He dribbled to his right and let fly with a jump shot from around 15 feet away. It was good! Time ran out. Bobby Plump's shot won the Indiana state championship for Milan.

Milan's entire population was 1,500. It is said that 40,000 people showed up the next day to celebrate. They were toasting something that will never happen again. Indiana high schools, like most states, now have divisions based on school size. No longer can David beat Goliath the way the Indians did in 1954. The newspapers called it the biggest sports story in Indiana history. It was the stuff that Hollywood dreams are made of.

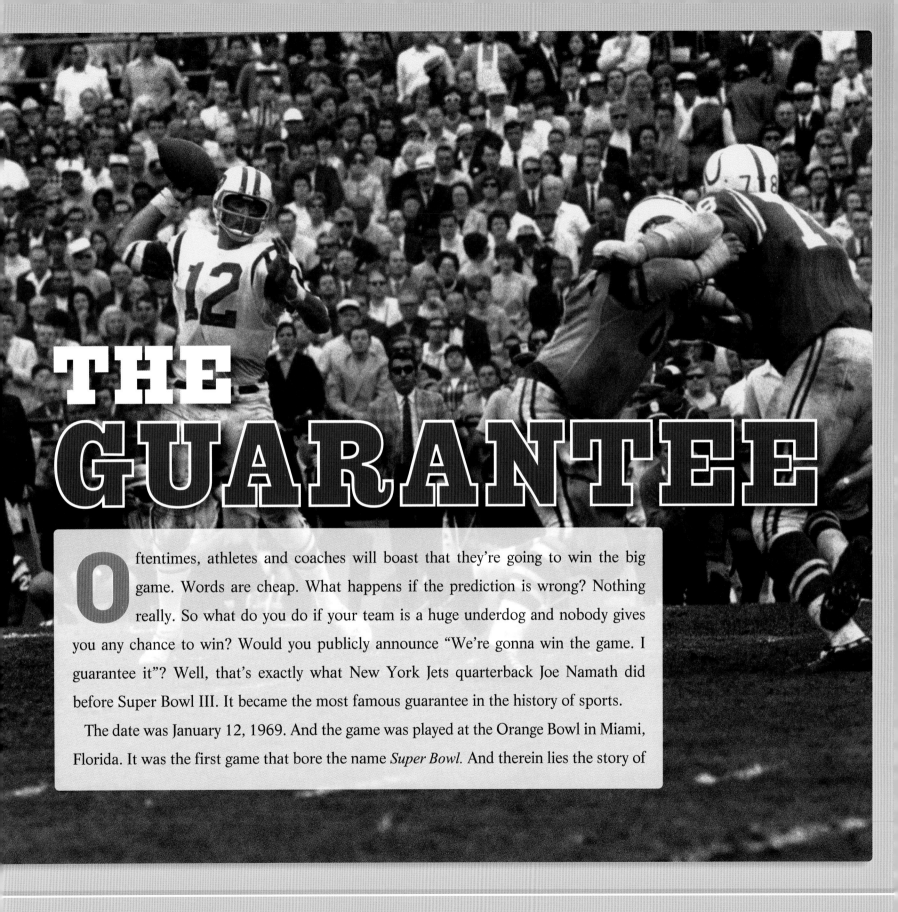

THE GUARANTEE

O ftentimes, athletes and coaches will boast that they're going to win the big game. Words are cheap. What happens if the prediction is wrong? Nothing really. So what do you do if your team is a huge underdog and nobody gives you any chance to win? Would you publicly announce "We're gonna win the game. I guarantee it"? Well, that's exactly what New York Jets quarterback Joe Namath did before Super Bowl III. It became the most famous guarantee in the history of sports.

The date was January 12, 1969. And the game was played at the Orange Bowl in Miami, Florida. It was the first game that bore the name *Super Bowl*. And therein lies the story of

JOE NAMATH

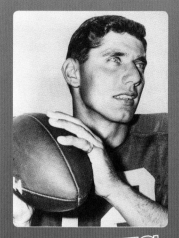

UPSETS AND UNDERDOGS

BORN: May 31, 1943

BIRTHPLACE: Beaver Falls, PA

HEIGHT: 6'2"

WEIGHT: 200 lbs.

TEAM: New York Jets

POSITION: Quarterback

THROWS: Right

CAREER PASSING YARDS: 27,663

PASSES COMPLETED: 1,886

ROOKIE YEAR: 1965

CAREER HIGHLIGHTS: Drafted by the New York Jets in the first round of the 1965 AFL Draft and by the St. Louis Cardinals in the first round of the 1965 NFL Draft; AFL MVP 1968 and 1969; Super Bowl III MVP in 1969.

The Titans played their home games at the old **POLO GROUNDS**, which had been home to the **NEW YORK GIANTS** baseball team before it moved to San Francisco. The **NEW YORK METS** also made it their home when they first came into existence.

why this game was such a big deal. The world of pro football was very different back then. The National Football League (NFL) came into existence in 1920. By the time the 1960s rolled around, thanks to television, it had become a hugely popular sport. In 1960 a rival league was formed, called the American Football League (AFL). One of the original teams in this upstart league was named the New York Titans.

The Titans weren't very good, and not many people showed up to watch them at their home stadium, the Polo Grounds. Attendance at Titans games was so sparse that they would ask the fans to move closer to the field so on TV it would look like there were a lot more people in the stands.

In 1964 the Titans found a new home and a new name. They would play in Shea Stadium, the newly built home of the New York Mets. Because Shea Stadium was situated right next to LaGuardia Airport, they changed the name from the Titans to the New York Jets. Still, attendance wasn't so hot, and the Jets—as well as the entire AFL—were considered inferior when compared with the older NFL.

But that all changed in 1965. On New Year's Day, Texas beat Alabama in the Orange Bowl 21–17. The losing Alabama quarterback was the talented Joe Namath, and despite the loss, he was named the game's Most Valuable Player (MVP). The very next day, he signed a contract that shocked the sports world. He was passing up the more established NFL to play in the AFL. He was paid an unheard of sum of $427,000, and he was promptly given the nickname "Broadway Joe."

Because of Joe's huge contract, NFL owners were worried that a bidding war would break out between the two rival leagues, so they worked out a peace plan. The two leagues agreed to have a combined draft of players so only one team could draft a player, not two teams in two separate leagues that would then bid against each other. The two rival leagues also agreed to play a championship game against

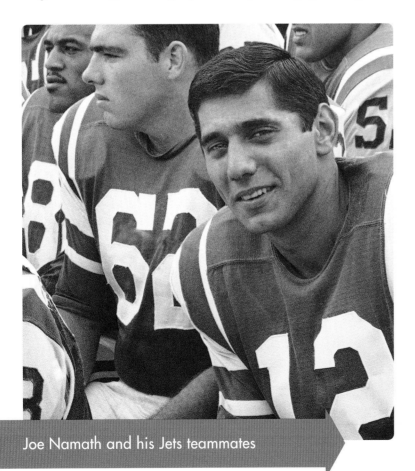

Joe Namath and his Jets teammates

each other at the end of the season. The first of those games was played in January of 1967, and it was called the AFL-NFL World Championship Game. The name *Super Bowl* wasn't used until two years later. In the first two AFL-NFL championship games, the Green Bay Packers entered the game as NFL champs. In the first championship game, the Packers easily beat the AFL champion Kansas City Chiefs, 35–10. The following year, they faced Oakland, and it was another easy Green Bay win, 33–14.

So against that backdrop, Super Bowl III would be played in 1969 between the NFL's Baltimore Colts and Joe Namath's New York Jets from the AFL. The leagues were still technically separate and wouldn't become one single league until 1970. And, of course, Baltimore was the heavy favorite to win the game. The Colts had the best record in all of football, 13–1. They had rolled up more than 400 points on offense, and their defense was the stingiest in the NFL, allowing the fewest points in the league. No wonder the oddsmakers predicted that the Colts would win the game by 18 points.

That brings us to "the Guarantee." Most experts felt that the Jets were lucky if they could keep the game close. Few, if any, thought they had a chance to actually win. One of those few was their quarterback, Joe Namath.

On the Thursday before the game, Joe was honored by the Miami Touchdown Club as the Player of the Year. At the dinner, a Colts fan yelled out that Baltimore was

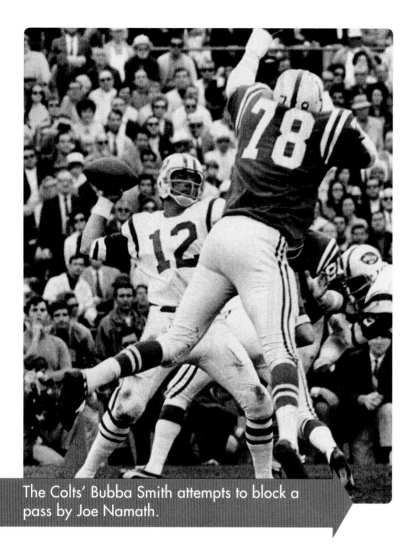

The Colts' Bubba Smith attempts to block a pass by Joe Namath.

"I've got news for you. We're gonna win the game. I guarantee it."

—JOE NAMATH

going to easily win the game. Namath shot back at the fan, "I've got news for you. We're gonna win the game. I guarantee it." Wow! Joe knew that every newspaper would be splashing that guarantee across its sports pages. Namath and his teammates had watched film of

the Colts, and they were confident they could beat them. But Coach Weeb Ewbank was furious. He knew that the Colts would use Joe's guarantee as motivation.

And then they kicked off the Super Bowl. The first time they got the ball, the Colts played like the heavy favorites that they were. Quarterback Earl Morrall passed to his tight end John Mackey, and Mackey ran over a couple of Jets defenders, gaining 19 yards. The Colts were rolling, right down to the Jets 19-yard line. It was then that New York's defense stiffened. Baltimore attempted a 27-yard field goal and missed. It was a sign of things to come. After the first quarter, the game was scoreless.

Baltimore threatened early in the second quarter, but Randy Beverly intercepted a pass in the end zone, and that's where the game turned around. The Jets took over on their own 20-yard line. Joe had a rifle arm, but at first he used it only to hand the ball off to his big fullback, Matt Snell. Snell pounded the Colts defense as the Jets marched down the field. Then Joe started to mix in some passes against that vaunted Baltimore defense.

Finally, Namath handed off to Snell, who rumbled into the end zone from four yards out. The Jets had held the ball for more than five minutes and driven 80 yards for the game's first score. The underdogs shockingly held a 7–0 lead. Baltimore missed another field goal, and the Jets made two more interceptions. It was still 7–0 New York at halftime.

The second half wasn't any better for Baltimore. On their very first play of the third quarter, the Colts fumbled. That led to a Jets field goal. The next time the Colts got the ball, they were forced to punt. That led to another Jets field goal. Suddenly the great Baltimore Colts found themselves trailing the underdog Jets 13–0. Early in the fourth quarter, the Jets upped their lead to 16–0.

The football world was being turned upside down. The Jets were so in command of the game that Namath didn't have to throw a single pass in the fourth quarter. He kept handing off to his running backs to run time off the clock. The Colts finally solved the Jets defense for a touchdown late in the fourth quarter, but it was too little too late. The Jets had done it: a stunning 16–7 victory!

Of course, Joe Namath was voted the game's MVP despite not having thrown a touchdown pass. In fact, he is the only quarterback to have won the Super Bowl MVP award without throwing a touchdown.

Each winning Jets player received $15,000, but they earned something a lot more valuable—newfound respect for the AFL. The "minor" league now had to be taken seriously. Joe and the Jets had done the impossible. They had thoroughly dismantled a team that was supposedly unbeatable. And why not? Watching the Colts on film had convinced Namath that the Jets would win—so much so that he "guaranteed it." To this day, it's considered the greatest upset in the history of pro football.

Joe Namath is the only quarterback to win the Super Bowl MVP award without throwing a touchdown pass.

THE MIRACLE ON THE MAT

f I mention the sport of wrestling, what do you think of? Perhaps some form of professional wrestling, which, as you probably know, isn't really a true sport. It's more of an entertainment show where many of the results are worked out in advance. But if you like to think of pro wrestling as a real sport, go ahead. It's very popular.

At the 2000 Olympics in Sydney, Australia, I was assigned to cover a Greco-Roman wrestling match. That was the first time I had ever seen the sport in person. And it turned out to be the biggest upset in the history of wrestling—if not the entire history of the Olympics.

How big of an upset was it? The match featured a dairy farmer from Wyoming named Rulon Gardner challenging the "Russian Bear," Aleksandr Karelin. Rulon had never won a major wrestling title. Karelin, on the other hand, had never lost one. He won the gold medal in the super heavyweight division at the 1988 Olympics in Seoul, South Korea. Then every year from 1989 to 1999, he either won the World Championships or the Olympics. He won two more gold medals at the 1992 Olympics in Barcelona, Spain, and the 1996 Olympics in Atlanta, Georgia.

And talk about a winning streak—Karelin had not lost a wrestling match in 13 years! For the last six of those years, opponents didn't score a single point against him. As a result, he is considered the greatest Greco-Roman wrestler of all time. You can understand why Rulon was a huge underdog when he walked onto the mat in Australia to face the Russian Bear.

The fact that Rulon was even able to walk onto the mat had to be considered a minor miracle in itself. He was born in the tiny town of Afton, Wyoming, the youngest of nine kids in his family. In 2000 the population of Afton was 1,818. There seemed to

A Greco-Roman wrestling match consists of two 3-minute periods.

With all that strength, Karelin developed a move called the "Karelin Lift." He would pick up his opponent, throw him down, and pin him to the mat. Wrestlers in lighter weight classes would use that maneuver, but it was unheard of in the super heavyweight division, where the wrestlers are at least 286 pounds. When he lifted his opponents, they were frightened, not only afraid of losing the match but also of getting seriously injured when Karelin threw them down.

As the Sydney Olympics competition unfolded, nobody

be a cloud hanging over young Rulon's head. When he was in the third grade, he brought an arrow to class for show and tell. He wound up puncturing his stomach with that arrow. Over the years, it was as if he had nine lives. He once got lost while snowmobiling and suffered frostbite. One of his toes had to be amputated. Another time, he got into a serious motorcycle accident. If that wasn't enough, he was a passenger in a small plane that crashed into a lake. Rulon had to swim for his life, and he wasn't a very good swimmer. But there was no cloud over his head that day in 2000, when he competed for the gold medal.

Karelin also had an interesting upbringing. He weighed 15 pounds when he was born. That is huge—and it was obviously a sign of things to come. He grew up in Siberia, Russia, where the temperature can easily reach 50 degrees below zero! He used that cold Siberian weather to his advantage. He would build up his strength by running through thigh-deep snow. He was so strong that he once carried a refrigerator up eight flights of stairs. No wonder they called him the Russian Bear!

Rulon Gardner of the United States holds Aleksandr Karelin of Russia during the 2000 Olympic Games in Sydney.

was surprised by the results. In the early rounds, Karelin wrestled four times and won all of his matches—two of them by pins. During the same rounds, Rulon Gardner also won all of his matches. But Rulon won on points. He didn't pin anyone.

On the day of the fateful final, Karelin had to wrestle two other matches—in the quarterfinals and semifinals. He easily won both without having a point scored against him.

Rulon Gardner had to wrestle only one other time that day—in the semifinals. His opponent, Juri Yevseychyc from Israel, gave him a tough match. Rulon trailed 2–0 with two minutes to go, but he found a way to tie it, forcing overtime. Yevseychyc was exhausted and stopped wrestling in the overtime period. Rulon was then awarded a point and the victory. It was on to the finals for Rulon Gardner against the unbeatable Aleksandr Karelin.

The date was September 7, 2000. One newspaper said the odds against Gardner winning were 2,000 to 1. The two of them had wrestled once before, in 1997, and Karelin had lifted Rulon three times, slamming him down to the mat twice. Karelin easily outpointed Rulon 5–0. The rematch was for Olympic gold.

During the first period, Karelin tried to lift Rulon, but unlike three years earlier, he was unable to execute his Karelin Lift. The period ended with no score. Under the rules of Greco-Roman wrestling, the second and final period begins in a clinch. Each wrestler holds his hands clasped tightly together. The wrestlers remain in that clinch position until one of them executes a scoring move or one of the wrestlers is forced to separate his hands. If the hands come apart, the opponent is awarded a point. And that's exactly what happened. It was ever so slight, but Karelin's hands appeared to separate.

JEFF BLATNICK was one of the announcers calling the match on television. He won the GOLD MEDAL for the UNITED STATES in GRECO-ROMAN WRESTLING in 1984. During the broadcast, he said that if Gardner were to win the match, it would be called "THE MIRACLE ON THE MAT."

The judges had to watch a TV replay to make sure it had really occurred. After a couple of minutes, they made their ruling. One point for Gardner. He led the match 1–0. How unusual was that? It was the first time in six years that anybody had scored a single point against the great Karelin. It was also the first time in 13 years that Karelin had trailed in a match.

Rulon Gardner smiles from the medal stand after winning the gold medal in 130 kg Greco-Roman wrestling.

But it wasn't over. They battled the rest of the second round, and that was the only score. But in Greco-Roman wrestling, participants can't win a match in just two rounds if they don't score at least three points, and Rulon had only scored one. So the match had to go into overtime—another three full minutes.

Rulon had the advantage on the scoreboard, but Karelin wasn't about to quit. He kept coming at Rulon, grabbing at him, trying to lift him up. And as the clock was ticking down, Rulon continued to get away from the Russian Bear. The crowd was chanting "U-S-A, U-S-A."

Finally, with just a few seconds remaining, Karelin stopped fighting. He conceded the match, and it was all over. Rulon Gardner had accomplished the impossible! He had handed Karelin his first career loss in international competition. Rulon's coach and his supporters immediately mobbed him. After the referee raised his arm in triumph, Rulon did a cartwheel, grabbed an American flag, and paraded it around the mat.

Then it was time for Rulon's TV interview. That's where I came in. It was my job to do the first interview with him after his historic win. During the interview, I was hoping to get Rulon to say how excited he was. I guess I wanted him to say something like, "This is the most unbelievable thing in the entire world, and I'm the greatest of all time!" But that wasn't his style. After about my fifth or sixth question, he simply stated matter-of-factly, "This is awesome." And it was. It was truly the "Miracle on the Mat."

THE MIRACLE METS

Two things happened in 1969. Well, actually, millions of things happened, but two really big things occurred. On July 20, 1969, an astronaut from Ohio named Neil Armstrong became the first human to take a stroll on the moon's surface. Less than 90 days later, a baseball team from Queens, New York, won the World Series. To this day, only one of the two events is referred to as a miracle.

There are lots of reasons why the Mets winning the 1969 World Series is considered remarkable. First off, it was just their eighth year of existence. When baseball teams are born, they normally don't have a lot of great players. It takes years to develop a championship team.

Not only were the Mets a new franchise, but during their first seven years, they were simply awful. In their first season, 1962, the Mets played 160 games and managed to lose 120 of them. In those days, there weren't divisions—just two leagues: the American and the National. The Mets finished dead last in the 10-team National League, a whopping 60½ games out of first. It's the worst record for any team in modern baseball history. Over the next five years, things improved for the Mets—but not by much. Four more 10th place finishes and two seasons in which they actually managed to climb out of the basement, finishing ninth!

The Mets became known as lovable losers. Their manager was Casey Stengel, who had managed the crosstown Yankees to seven World Series titles. Stengel was a colorful character who often said funny things. So while the Mets were losing, he would make things humorous with some great quotes. He once said "The only thing worse than a Mets game is a Mets doubleheader."

If you had to pick one player who symbolized the Mets in those early days, it was Marv Throneberry. His middle name was Eugene, so his initials spelled out MET. Perfect.

"Been in this game 100 years, but I see new ways to lose 'em I never knew existed before."

—CASEY STENGEL

He picked up the nickname "Marvelous Marv," but he was anything but. He wasn't a very good fielder, but he may have been equally bad as a base runner. One play stands out. Throneberry hit what looked like a game-winning triple—but he was called out because he failed to touch first base. It was the third out of the inning. When Casey Stengel came out to argue with the umps, they told him to hold his breath—Throneberry had also missed second!

The 1969 New York Mets

Karl Ehrhardt, the Mets fan known as Sign Man

But while the Mets were a laughingstock on the field, they slowly started to acquire some key players, especially pitchers. In 1964 they signed a lefty from Minnesota: Jerry Koosman. He turned out to be one of the best pitchers they ever had. The following year, they drafted a hard-throwing righty from Texas named Nolan Ryan. Ryan would go on to become one of the greatest pitchers in the history of baseball. The year after drafting Ryan, their biggest signing was a pitcher from California, Tom Seaver. Seaver, like Ryan, would wind up in the Baseball Hall of Fame. In addition to building a strong roster, in 1968 the Mets hired former Brooklyn Dodgers star Gil Hodges to be their manager. The following season, everything clicked.

In 1969 the Mets were finally guaranteed *not* to finish ninth or 10th for the first time in their history. That's because the National League expanded to 12 teams, adding Montreal and San Diego. The 12 teams in the National League were split into two divisions: the East and the West. The worst the Mets could now do was finish sixth in the National League East.

The way the 1969 season unfolded, nobody could have guessed what was about to take place. On August 13, the Mets trailed the first place Chicago Cubs by 9½ games. And that was the moment everything turned around. They won both ends of two doubleheaders on consecutive days against San Diego. I guess Casey Stengel was wrong about Mets doubleheaders. Then they had to face the Giants future Hall of Fame pitcher, Juan Marichal. There was no score in the 14th inning, and Marichal was still pitching for the Giants. In the bottom of the 14th, Tommie Agee hit a homer and won the game for the Mets. They were now on a tear. In a 16-game stretch, the Mets won 14 games!

On September 9, the Mets beat the Cubs 7–1 to cut Chicago's lead to half a game. Are you superstitious? During that game, a black cat wandered near the Cubs

FAST FACT

The year that the Mets came into being, so did the Houston Colt .45s, who are now known as the Houston Astros. They have yet to win a World Series, and they've been around for more than 50 seasons.

on-deck circle. The next day, the Mets won a doubleheader, the Cubs lost, and the Mets took over first place for good. It was the first time in their entire history that they were in first. On the night of September 23, the Mets beat St. Louis 3–2 and clinched the National League East. Delirious fans swarmed onto the field at Shea Stadium. When the regular season ended, Tom Seaver had 25 wins, the most of any pitcher in the majors. And the team that had never won more than 73 games in a season had won 100!

In 1969, for the first time, there were division playoffs before the World Series. The Mets had to face the Atlanta Braves for the National League pennant. The Braves were led by the great Hank Aaron, who five years later would break Babe Ruth's all-time home run record. It was a best-of-five series. Even though Aaron hit a home run in

Mets pitcher Jerry Koosman delivers a left-handed pitch against the Orioles.

"You look up and down the bench and you have to say to yourself, 'Can't anybody here play this game?'"

—CASEY STENGEL

each of the three games, the upstart Mets were on a roll. They swept the Braves 3–0 and charged into the 1969 World Series.

Waiting for them were the Baltimore Orioles, the team many considered to be the best in baseball. The Orioles featured four future Hall of Famers: right fielder Frank Robinson, third baseman Brooks Robinson, pitcher Jim Palmer, and manager Earl Weaver. Most experts predicted that the Orioles would win. In Game 1, they didn't disappoint. Mike Cuellar outdueled Tom Seaver, and Baltimore won 4–1. It was the Orioles last hurrah. The Mets evened the series the next day by pushing across a run in the ninth to win 2–1.

On October 14, 1969, the World Series arrived at Shea Stadium for the first time. The Mets dominated. The first batter for the Mets, Tommie Agee, blasted a long home run to center field off Jim Palmer. Quickly, it was 1–0 Mets and then Agee proceeded to put on a show in center field. In the fourth inning, two Orioles on base, he made a terrific running catch in deep left-center. In the seventh, with the bases loaded, he made an even better diving catch in deep right-center. With those two catches, Agee saved five runs, and the Mets won Game 3, 5–0.

In Game 4, there were more heroics. Tom Seaver pitched great, and right fielder Ron Swoboda made an amazing diving catch in the ninth inning. The Mets won a 10-inning squeaker, 2–1. Suddenly the underdogs led 3–1 in the series.

Game 5 featured another crazy moment. The Mets were trailing 3–0 in the sixth when Orioles pitcher Dave McNally bounced a pitch to Cleon Jones. The Mets claimed that the ball hit Jones's shoe. Mets manager Gil Hodges pointed to shoe polish on the baseball to prove it. The umps agreed and awarded Jones first base. The next batter, Donn Clendenon, hit a two-run homer, and the Mets were on their way. It was 5–3 Mets in the top of the ninth with

a runner on first, two outs, and Jerry Koosman on the mound. Baltimore's Davey Johnson hit a long fly ball to left. A homer would tie the game, but Cleon Jones settled under it and made the catch. It was mayhem. The Mets jumped on top of each other, and again, the fans ran onto

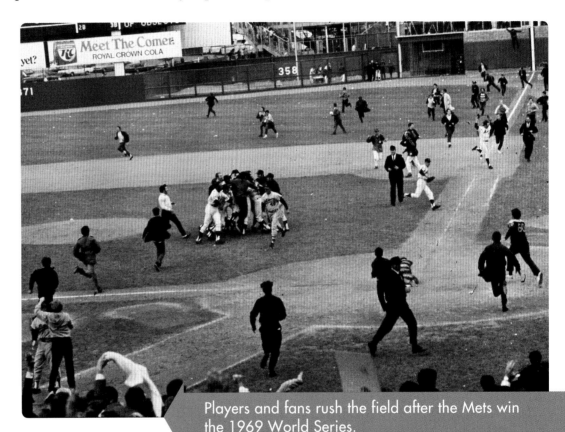

Players and fans rush the field after the Mets win the 1969 World Series.

the field. The Mets had done the inconceivable. They had shocked the baseball world by beating Baltimore and winning the World Series 4 games to 1.

To honor the champs, there was a ticker tape parade in New York City. A miracle had truly happened. Mets fans were over the moon.

Betting on sports events is legal in Las Vegas, Nevada. The casinos will take bets on just about anything. But when Mike Tyson was scheduled to box Buster Douglas, almost all the casinos refused to post any odds. The betting experts thought it was a complete mismatch and that Tyson would easily win. And why wouldn't they think that? Tyson was considered unstoppable. He had fought 37 times in his career, and he had won every fight—most by knockout. He wasn't the tallest or heaviest of boxers, just the most feared—so much so that only one Las Vegas casino decided to post odds for his fight against Douglas. That casino installed Mike as an overwhelming 42–1 favorite.

Mike Tyson grew up in a tough neighborhood in Brooklyn, New York. He was often the target of bullying, so he learned to fight at an early age. And he was constantly getting into trouble. By the time he was a teenager, he had been arrested more than 30 times. As a result, he was sent away to a reform school, and that's where he really learned to fight. A counselor at the reform school, Bobby Stewart, was a former amateur boxing champion. He agreed to teach young Mike to fight if Mike would apply himself at school. Both of them kept their ends of the bargain.

The more Mike trained, the better he got. Eventually, he moved out of the reform school and in with legendary boxing manager Cus D'Amato. He went to high school during the day, and he trained every night. At age 18, Mike was ready. He was about to take the boxing world by storm.

His first professional fight was in Albany, New York, on March 6, 1985, against a fighter named Hector Mercedes. Mike wasted little time and knocked him out in the

LISTEN to this MOMENT TRACK 3

Boxing promoter Don King lifts heavyweight champion Mike Tyson.

calling him "the baddest man on the planet." The next year was even better. He kept fighting and kept winning. He was now 27–0, and almost all of his wins had come by knockout. He was finally ready for the next step.

On November 22, 1986, in Las Vegas, Mike fought Trevor Berbick for the heavyweight title. Berbick was the World Boxing Council (WBC) heavyweight champion—and he didn't last two rounds. Mike staggered him at the end of the first round and then knocked him down in the opening minute of the second. Later in the round, Mike knocked him down a second time. Berbick tried to get up, but he couldn't. It was over. Mike Tyson was the new WBC Heavyweight Champion of the world. He was just 20 years old—the youngest heavyweight champ in boxing history. Within six months, he also won the World Boxing Association (WBA) and International Boxing Federation (IBF) championships. He was the first boxer to ever wear all three championship belts at the same time!

Mike continued to fight, putting all his titles on the line six more times. Two of those fights were against former heavyweight champions Larry Holmes and Michael Spinks. He knocked out Holmes in the fourth round and Spinks in the first! The "baddest man on the planet" could not be stopped. By 1990 he was 37–0, and he had won 33 of his fights by knockout.

Meanwhile, James "Buster" Douglas grew up in

first round. It was a sign of things to come. For the rest of the year, he fought at least once a month—sometimes twice or even three times. By the end of 1985, Mike had fought 15 opponents and had beaten all of them. Eleven of the fights ended in the first round! He quickly picked up the nickname "Iron Mike," and some people started

"IRON" MIKE TYSON JAMES "BUSTER" DOUGLAS

BORN: June 30, 1966
HOMETOWN: Brooklyn, NY
HEIGHT: 5'10"
WEIGHT: 220 lbs.
REACH: 71"
LIFETIME RECORD: 50–6

BORN: April 7,1960
HOMETOWN: Columbus, OH
HEIGHT: 6'3½"
WEIGHT: 231 lbs.
REACH: 83"
LIFETIME RECORD: 38–6

Columbus, Ohio. His dad was a professional fighter named William "Dynamite" Douglas. It seemed as if Buster was born to be a boxer. But in high school, he turned to other sports. He was good at football and basketball. He even helped his high school basketball team win the Ohio state championship. After a few years of playing college basketball, Buster returned home and asked his dad to train him in boxing.

Buster was big and strong, and in his first 20 fights, he only lost once. Then again, he didn't fight anyone noteworthy. The scouting report on Buster said that he had talent but didn't always train hard. Boxing insiders claimed he lacked "heart." In their eyes, he just didn't seem to give 100 percent effort. He eventually started fighting some better opponents, and in 1987, he fought for the IBF heavyweight title against Tony Tucker and lost. So when

he was chosen to fight Mike Tyson in February 1990, boxing experts thought he'd be easy pickings for Iron Mike.

Buster's record was 29–4–1 with 19 knockouts. It looked pretty impressive on paper, but everyone knew that most of those wins were against easy opponents, especially when compared with Mike. And that's why hardly any boxing fans or oddsmakers thought Buster had a prayer.

Buster was 29 years old—six years older than Mike. He was also 5 inches taller and 11 pounds heavier, and his reach was a whole foot longer than Mike's. And still, with all those physical advantages, the aggressive Mike Tyson was expected to easily defeat Douglas. In fact, so many people thought Buster was going to lose that not one photographer showed up for his prefight weigh-in.

The fight was set for February 11, 1990, in Tokyo, Japan. Buster committed himself to his training regimen.

He was in terrific shape—but just 23 days before the fight, his mother died. It gave boxing fans one more reason to think Buster's heart wouldn't be in it.

As the fight got under way, Buster Douglas looked good. In fact, through the first couple of rounds, he landed more punches than Mike. Already, that was highly unusual. Many of Mike Tyson's fights didn't even last a couple of rounds. Buster's height and reach started to pay off, and by the fifth round, to the shock of everyone, he was dominating the fight.

Mike really wasn't doing much of anything, which was very uncharacteristic for him. But then at the end of the eighth round, he unloaded one of his classic uppercuts and connected. Douglas went down! The ref was counting—"...six, seven, eight, nine..."—but Buster popped back up on his feet. He had barely beaten the 10 count to stay alive. Just then, the bell sounded to end the eighth round.

As the ninth round began, Mike went in for the kill, but Buster fought him off. In fact, Buster did more than just play defense—he went back on the attack and staggered Mike. With a minute to go in the round, it didn't look like Iron Mike would survive. Buster was

Buster Douglas finishes Mike Tyson with a left.

all over him, and Mike was backed up against the ropes. Mike appeared tired and worn out as the bell sounded to end the ninth round.

Then it happened. It was so unexpected because it had never happened before. About a minute into the 10th round, Buster connected with a mighty uppercut and then a three-punch combination: left, right, left. The right hand missed, but the two lefts connected solidly. On the second one, Mike Tyson went down to the canvas. It was the first time in his career that he had ever been knocked down. He tried to get up, but he couldn't. And just like that, it was over. The ferocious fighter who had never lost a fight had been knocked out.

Buster's cornermen rushed into the ring to hug the new champion. He was asked what had inspired him to beat Mike Tyson, and Buster answered, "My mother, my mother. God bless her heart." Contrary to belief, his mom's passing away had given him added inspiration.

The TV announcers were amazed at what they had

Buster Douglas raises his glove after a tenth round knockout against Mike Tyson.

Buster Douglas helped kick off the 1990 Ohio State Fair. One special feature of the state fair that year was a life-sized sculpture of the world heavyweight champion made from butter.

seen. One of them called it "the greatest upset in boxing history." It was hard to disagree.

THE MIRACLE ON ICE

Every one of these stories tells of improbable results. They all have something in common. The eventual winner was a major underdog and yet each climbed to the heights. Is one comeback or upset greater than the next? It's hard to compare. But after you read about the U.S. Olympic hockey team, you might argue that their story is the greatest upset in the history of American sports.

On February 9, 1980, the U.S. Olympic hockey team played an exhibition game against the mighty Soviet Union at Madison Square Garden. The game was played three days before the opening ceremony for the Lake Placid, New York, Olympics. It was a slaughter. The Soviets embarrassed the Americans 10–3. Nobody was surprised. The Soviets had won the gold medal in hockey at the previous four Olympics. They were an unbeatable powerhouse.

On my TV sportscast that night in New York, I proclaimed, "Why even bother playing the Olympic hockey tournament at Lake Placid? Just wrap up the gold medals and ship them to Russia." It was probably the dumbest thing I ever said on television. Nobody could have predicted what would happen 13 days later—least of all me.

Things were very different back in 1980. National Hockey League players weren't allowed to participate in the Olympics because they are professionals. That rule has been changed, so NHL stars now can play Olympic hockey. But because of that rule, the 1980 American Olympic hockey team consisted of a bunch of college players whose average age was just 22. They were chosen in the months before the Olympics and didn't have much time to practice or play together.

On the other hand, the Soviet team was the best national team in the world. The players stayed together for years, and they trained year-round. That's why it was hardly surprising when they won that exhibition game 10–3 before the 1980 Olympics began.

The coach of the U.S. hockey team was Herb Brooks. He had played for the United States in the Olympics and was the successful hockey coach at the University of Minnesota. In 1979 his Minnesota Gophers won the national championship in college hockey, so when it came

Robert McClanahan of the U.S. slams into Aleksandr Golikov of the Soviet team during the Olympics playoff game.

time to pick the 20 hockey players who would represent the United States in the Olympics, he chose lots of players he knew. Twelve of the 20 players were born in the state of Minnesota, and nine of those 12 had played for Brooks at the University of Minnesota.

Brooks was a tough taskmaster and worked the kids hard. He had conditioning drills that became known as "Herbies." He would make his players skate wind sprints back and

forth on the ice until they were ready to drop. Leading up to the Olympics, they played 61 exhibition games against all sorts of competition. After a 4–4 tie with Norway, Brooks wasn't happy with the team's effort, so after the game was over, he made the players go back onto the ice. By now, fans had left the stadium, and Brooks had his team do Herbies over and over. It went on so long that they turned off the lights in the arena. The U.S. hockey team did Herbies in the dark! The players hated it, but it whipped them into terrific shape.

There were 12 teams in the Olympic hockey tournament. The United States was seeded seventh, which meant they were a long shot to win a medal of any color. The first game was against Sweden, and with just 27 seconds left, Bill Baker scored to give the Americans a 2–2 tie. Not a bad start—the Swedes were ranked number three. But now awaiting the United States was a talented Czechoslovakian team that was seeded second. That game produced the first shocker. The American kids won convincingly, 7–3. Something was brewing.

Then the United States beat Norway and Romania. If they could beat West Germany, they would get into the medal round. They quickly fell behind 2–0 in the first period, but they came roaring back to win 4–2. The team that was seeded seventh had made it to the final four. One more victory and they were guaranteed to win a medal.

But standing in the way was the mighty Soviet team—the same one that had totally humiliated them 13 days earlier. On top of that, the Soviets had been just as unbeatable in the 1980 Olympics. They crushed Japan 16–0 and trounced the Netherlands 17–4.

Suddenly the United States was a nation of hockey fans. Even if people had never seen a hockey game in their lives, it seemed as if everyone was captivated by this group of kids who were doing amazing things. If you ask people who were alive back then, I'm guessing they'll be able to tell you exactly where they were when that game was played.

On February 22, 1980, before the U.S. team took to the ice, Herb Brooks told them, "You were born to be hockey players. You were meant to be here. This moment is yours."

And that it was. They certainly had the home-ice advantage. Fans in the packed arena were waving huge American flags. But as usual, the U.S. team fell behind. The Soviets scored the first goal of the game, and after the Americans tied it, the Soviets took a 2–1 lead. Then as the final seconds ticked down in the first period, Dave Christian shot the puck from about 100 feet away. The rebound came right to Mark Johnson, and he scored with just one second to go in the first period. The underdogs had tied the game 2–2 after one period of play.

The Soviets dominated the second period—in fact, they dominated on offense for most of the game. But U.S. goalie Jim Craig was up to the task. In that second

U.S. goalie Jim Craig defends the goal against the Russian team.

period, the Soviets took 12 shots on goal to just two for the Americans. Craig stopped all but one. After two periods, the Soviets led 3–2. They would never score again.

With eight-and-a-half minutes gone in the third period, Mark Johnson scored his second goal of the game to tie the score 3–3. The arena was going crazy. Fans were chanting "U-S-A, U-S-A" as the scrappy American kids were now even with the heavily favored Soviets. And then it happened. Exactly halfway through the third period, Mike Eruzione took a low shot, and he scored! Eruzione danced a little jig on the ice. His teammates mobbed him.

It was sheer bedlam in the arena. For the first time in the game, the United States had taken the lead, 4–3. But there were still 10 long minutes to go.

For fans of the U.S. hockey team, those were the longest 10 minutes ever. The Soviets were desperate to tie the game, but Jim Craig continued to stand tall in goal. The Soviets kept scrambling, but as the clock ticked down, the U.S. team maintained its slim 4–3 lead. Finally there was less than a minute to go and then 30 seconds. The announcer on TV was Al Michaels. Here's his call of the final frantic moments:

Eleven seconds. You've got 10 seconds. The countdown is going on right now. [Ken] Morrow up to [Dave] Silk. Five seconds left in the game...Do you believe in miracles? Yes!

It's one of the most famous play-by-play calls ever made, as befits one of the greatest upsets in the history of sports. The players all jumped onto the ice, threw their sticks and gloves in the air, and mobbed Jim Craig. As the U.S. players hugged, the Soviets just stood there in stunned disbelief.

Fans in the arena and around the country started to celebrate. They waved American flags. Everybody was feeling patriotic. These kids had done the unbelievable.

But there was one slight problem. The team had to play one more game two days later against Finland for the gold medal. Yes, they fell behind once again before coming back to win 4–2. They had struck gold!

When it was time to receive their medals, there was only room on the podium for the team captain, Mike Eruzione. But he motioned for all his teammates to join him, which they did. It was a magnificent team effort. They had accomplished the unthinkable. It was truly a miracle on ice.

The 1980 U.S. hockey team celebrates its gold medal victory.

ONE GOLDEN MOMENT

Can you ever say that someone was born to do something? I would like to suggest that Sarah Hughes was born to ice-skate. She was the fourth of six kids in her family, and skating is what her older brothers and sisters did. They grew up in the New York City suburb of Great Neck, Long Island. And it's not like everyone in her town was ice-skating. Then again, not everyone had John Hughes for a father. John is from Canada, where skating and playing hockey are national passions. John was the captain of the Cornell hockey team in 1970 when it went undefeated and won the national championship. He built a skating rink in the backyard so the kids could skate whenever they wanted. That's why Sarah was lacing up ice skates at age three.

One night 13 years later, she skated for a total of four minutes in Salt Lake City, Utah. What happened during those four short minutes is considered one of the greatest upsets in the history of Olympic figure skating.

Figure skating is a lot more than just looking graceful and skating around the ice. As the years have gone by, skaters have learned to execute more and more difficult moves. There's the axel jump, where a skater jumps up from one skate, spins 1½ times in the air, and lands on the other skate. Then there's a move called the Salchow, which also involves lifting off on one foot, spinning in the air, and landing on the other. A toe loop is where the skater jumps off on one skate and lands on the same skate. By the time Sarah was five, she could do all these, including

LISTEN to this MOMENT TRACK 4

double Salchows, which means she was rotating in midair twice before landing.

Not surprisingly, Sarah won local competitions, collected trophies, and built confidence in herself. When she was eight years old, she went on television and said, "I want to win a gold medal in the Olympics. I can't wait for that to happen." She was nine when she started working with coach Robin Wagner, a former figure skater. Three years later, Sarah won the junior U.S. title. She was all of 12 years old.

Sarah stepped up to the senior division at age 13. She was the youngest skater at the world championships, finishing seventh. The following year, in 2000, she moved up to fifth. And then in 2001, at age 15, she won the bronze medal. She was getting better and better. In November 2001, she won her first major title, Skate Canada. Not only did she take home gold, but she beat the big stars of her sport for the first time—fellow American Michelle Kwan and Irina Slutskaya of Russia.

Now it was on to Los Angeles, California, for the U.S. Figure Skating Championships in January. It was time to crown the American champion for 2002. In addition, the event would determine which three young women would make the U.S. Olympic figure skating team. As expected, 21-year-old Michelle Kwan won the gold medal. It was her sixth national title. Seventeen-year-old Sasha Cohen grabbed the silver and 16-year-old Sarah Hughes took

Winning the U.S. Junior Championships sometimes meant female skaters fell under the **"JUNIOR LADY CURSE."** Before Sarah Hughes, only two women—**TENLEY ALBRIGHT** and **CAROL HEISS**—won the U.S. Junior Championships and then went on to win Olympic gold—and they won those junior championships way back in the 1950s.

SARAH HUGHES

BORN: May 2, 1985

BIRTHPLACE: Great Neck, New York

HEIGHT: 5'5"

CAREER HIGHLIGHTS:
Landed a record-setting seven triple jumps to win Olympic Gold in 2002

UPSETS AND UNDERDOGS

home the bronze. The Olympics were now one month away on American soil in Salt Lake City.

If an American figure skater were to win the gold in Salt Lake, it would surely have to be Michelle Kwan. She had won the silver medal at the 1998 Olympics, and she was the two-time defending world champion. She and Irina Slutskaya were considered the heavy favorites. It bothered Sarah that she was being ignored. Nobody thought the 16-year-old from Great Neck had a chance.

There are two parts to Olympic figure skating. First, the women skate a short program, which counts for one-third of the final score. A few days later, it's the free skate, or long program, which counts for the other two-thirds. On February 19, 2002, the women competed in the short program. Sarah Hughes was nervous as she made her Olympic debut. When it was over, she was in fourth place. Michelle Kwan, as expected, was first. Then came Irina Slutskaya, and in third was Sasha Cohen. In the history of women's Olympic figure skating, nobody had ever gone from fourth place after the short program to win the gold medal.

It was Thursday night, February 21. By her own admission, Sarah had little expectation of winning the gold medal. The pressure was off of her because nobody thought she would win. So she wasn't going to hold back. She would go all out for every second she was on the ice. Her plan was to just skate and have fun. But Sarah did much more than that.

As she took the ice, she had a big smile on her face. She was so relaxed. And then her program began. Sarah started skating gracefully, slowly working up toward the difficult jumps she was about to attempt. One by one, she performed her jumps, nailing each one perfectly to the delight of the crowd. In all, she attempted seven triple jumps—four of them in combinations of two, or what is known as a triple-triple. No woman had ever attempted two triple-triples in a single program. Sarah not only attempted them, but she performed them flawlessly.

One of the announcers on television gushed that "...this is the kind of performance you just dream about." When it was over, Sarah herself looked like she couldn't believe

Sarah Hughes performs her routine in the women's free-skating program at the 2002 Olympics.

by one, the top skaters took the ice, and one by one, they didn't match up to Sarah's performance. Sasha Cohen fell while attempting one of her triple jumps. Next up, the favorite, Michelle Kwan, also fell on a triple jump. Suddenly Sarah Hughes was looking better and better. Now there was just one skater to go—Irina Slutskaya. Irina skated well, but her program wasn't as difficult as Sarah's. She also made some minor mistakes, and she nearly fell during one of her landings.

It was now in the hands of the judges, and in the complicated world of figure skating scoring, nobody had any idea who was going to win. The TV cameras were focused on Sarah and Robin Wagner as they sat quietly in an empty locker room, waiting for the final result. Sarah would have been happy with a bronze medal.

But the amazing happened. The scores flashed. Sarah had won the gold! The dreams of an eight-year-old had come true. Sarah and Robin started hugging and screaming, and they fell to the floor, shouting "Oh my gosh!" They couldn't believe it. Nobody could.

Back home in Great Neck, New York, where she had started skating in her backyard as a three-year-old, a big parade was staged in her honor. And why not? At the tender age of 16, on the world's biggest stage, she had skated beautifully. She had shocked the world to become an Olympic champion. What else could she possibly want? Sarah had an answer. She wanted to get her driver's license!

it. She skated over and collapsed in tears in her coach Robin Wagner's arms. When the judges' scores were announced, the cheers of the crowd exploded even louder. She had moved into first place. But the three top skaters had yet to take the ice.

All Sarah and Robin could do was sit back and wait. And what happened next was almost unimaginable. One

NEARLY PERFECT

Perfection in sports doesn't come around very often. In the past 100 years or so, there have been hundreds of thousands of Major League Baseball games, but pitchers have thrown less than 25 perfect games. That's where a pitcher retires all 27 hitters that he faces. It's only happened once in the World Series: Don Larsen for the New York Yankees against the Brooklyn Dodgers in 1956. In gymnastics, Nadia Comeneci of Romania scored the first perfect 10 in Olympic history in Montreal in 1976. But they've since changed the scoring rules in gymnastics, and there's no such thing as a perfect 10 anymore.

So it was possible for a pitcher and a gymnast to be perfect, but could a team be perfect for an entire season? There have been many college basketball and football teams that have gone complete seasons without losing a game. But how about the National Football League (NFL)? Only the 1972 Miami Dolphins never lost a game. They finished the regular season 14–0, won two playoff games, and then won the Super Bowl to finish with a perfect 17–0 record. Nobody has done it since. This is the story of a team that actually did better than 17–0: the 2007 New England Patriots.

Because their season was two games longer than the 1972 Dolphins, the Patriots finished the regular season 16–0. They also won two playoff games. So they were 18–0. But their season wasn't over. They still had to play in the Super Bowl. They were heavy favorites to beat the New York Giants and end their season 19–0. That's what most

Giants quarterback Eli Manning passes against Patriots defense during Super Bowl XLII.

experts predicted would happen. But as you've seen so far in this book, the experts can be spectacularly wrong.

In the decade of 2000, the New England Patriots were the best team in the NFL. Led by a terrific quarterback, Tom Brady, and a smart coach in Bill Belichick, they made it to three Super Bowls between 2002 and 2005. They won all three. Brady was the Most Valuable Player (MVP) in two of them. So when the Patriots got off to a good start in 2007, nobody was surprised.

In fact, their start was scary good. They scored exactly 38 points in each of their first three games against the New York Jets, the San Diego Chargers, and the Buffalo Bills. They easily won all three. They scored 34 points in each of their next two games. Two more wins. So not only were they winning, they were consistent.

And then they exploded. Against Dallas, Brady threw five touchdown passes and the Patriots beat the Cowboys 48–27. The next week, Brady went one better—six touchdown passes as the Patriots beat Miami 49–27. And the following week, the high-powered Patriots offense scored more than 50 points as they crushed Washington 52–7. The season was now half over, and the Patriots were a perfect 8–0. They didn't come close to losing.

For their ninth game, they beat star quarterback Peyton Manning and the Indianapolis Colts 24–20. The streak nearly came to an end

TOM BRADY

VS

ELI MANNING

BORN: August 3, 1977

HEIGHT: 6'4"

WEIGHT: 225 lbs.

2007 SEASON STATS

PASSING YARDS: 4,806—career high

TOUCHDOWNS: 50—NFL record

INTERCEPTIONS: 8

4TH SUPER BOWL APPEARANCE

1ST SUPER BOWL APPEARANCE

BORN: January 3, 1981

HEIGHT: 6'4"

WEIGHT: 218 lbs.

2007 SEASON STATS

PASSING YARDS: 3,336

TOUCHDOWNS: 23

INTERCEPTIONS: 20

when the Patriots played the Philadelphia Eagles, but a fourth-quarter touchdown enabled New England to run its record to 11–0. The following week, it was the same story in Baltimore: the Patriots trailed the Ravens in the fourth quarter, but Tom Brady led them to yet another comeback win. Could this be the team that would finally break the 1972 Miami Dolphins record? It was certainly starting to look that way.

Week after week, win after win, the Patriots breezed to a 15–0 record. There was just one more regular-season game to go—against the New York Giants. At this point, both the Giants and the Patriots had clinched playoff spots. Even though the game had little meaning for the Giants,

they went all out trying to end the Patriots winning streak.

In the third quarter, the Giants led the Patriots 28–16. But Brady did it again—he engineered yet another comeback, and New England won it 38–35. The Patriots had now done what no other team had accomplished. They had gone 16–0 in the regular season. They had the best offense in all of football, and their defense was strong too. Perfection was now within their grasp. All they had to do was win two playoff games and then the Super Bowl to complete an unprecedented 19–0 season.

The Patriots easily defeated Jacksonville and San Diego in the playoffs and arrived at Super Bowl XLII in Glendale, Arizona, at 18–0. And who was waiting for them? The same New York Giants who had played so well only to lose in that final regular-season game.

The Giants were a surprise. Their regular-season record was just 10–6, and they had finished three games behind Dallas in the NFC East. The Giants got into the playoffs as a wild card. While the Patriots had the best offense in football, the Giants were ranked 14th out of 32 teams. The Patriots were fourth in the league on defense, but the Giants were only 17th. In other words, the Giants were a very average team statistically when stacked up against the mighty Patriots.

The telecast of **SUPER BOWL XLII** on Fox broke the record for the **MOST WATCHED** Super Bowl in history with an average of **97.5 MILLION** viewers in the United States.

But once in the playoffs, the Giants caught fire. They had to play three games on the road, which is the hardest path a team can take. First they won in Tampa Bay and then they won in Dallas. Only the Green Bay Packers stood between the Giants and the Super Bowl. On a freezing Sunday night in Green Bay, Wisconsin, the teams played a thrilling NFC Championship Game. How cold was it? It was –7 degrees and the wind chill factor made it feel like –27. I was there, and I was never so cold in my life. In overtime, Lawrence Tynes kicked a 47-yard field goal, giving the Giants a 23–20 win! It was on to Super Bowl XLII in much warmer Arizona and a date with the undefeated AFC champs: the New England Patriots.

For the big game, the Giants were considered the underdogs, and their strategy was simple: keep the ball for a long time on offense so Tom Brady couldn't get onto the field. And when Brady got in there, the plan was to pressure him relentlessly.

It started well for the Giants. They took the opening kickoff and kept the ball for 10 minutes. They wound up kicking a field goal. But when the Patriots got the ball, they also drove down the field. On the first play of the second quarter, Laurence Maroney scored a one-yard touchdown. The Patriots led 7–3. And then nobody scored again until the fourth quarter.

The Giants defense continued to hound Brady, hitting him often and sacking him five times. Early in the fourth quarter, Giants quarterback Eli Manning, the younger brother of Colts star Peyton Manning, threw a five-yard touchdown pass to a little-used wide receiver named David Tyree. The Giants had a 10–7 lead. It was Tyree's first touchdown catch all season. Back came the Patriots. With 2:45 left in the game, Brady hit Randy Moss with a seven-yard touchdown pass. New England was back on top 14–10.

The Giants appeared doomed. But in the nick of time

New York Giants Eli Manning scrambles to pass on the way to Super Bowl victory.

Eli Manning celebrates a Super Bowl win for the Giants.

they pulled off one of the most unbelievable plays in Super Bowl history. With just 1:15 left in the game, the Giants faced a third down and five yards to go on their own 44-yard line. Manning took the snap and started scrambling around. He was in trouble. The Patriots were grabbing at him and pulling on his jersey, and it looked as if he might be tackled, but Manning somehow got away from his pursuers and flung the ball far downfield. There, once again, was David Tyree. He and Patriots defensive back Rodney Harrison both jumped high into the air to try to catch the ball. But it was Tyree who grabbed the ball in midair and pinned it against his helmet with his right hand while falling backward to the ground on top of Harrison. It was amazing.

The play gained 33 yards and is arguably the greatest catch in Super Bowl history.

Four plays later, Manning threw a 13-yard touchdown pass to Plaxico Burress with just 35 seconds left in the game. The underdog Giants had taken the lead 17–14. Brady had one last chance, but he had run out of comebacks. The Giants shocked everyone and beat the unbeatable Patriots to win the championship. They held a ticker tape parade in New York City to honor the Giants. As for the Patriots, they finished their season 18–1—one of the best records ever but still disappointing. Perhaps they were comforted in the knowledge that it took a miraculous catch to prevent them from attaining perfection.

MARCH MADNESS

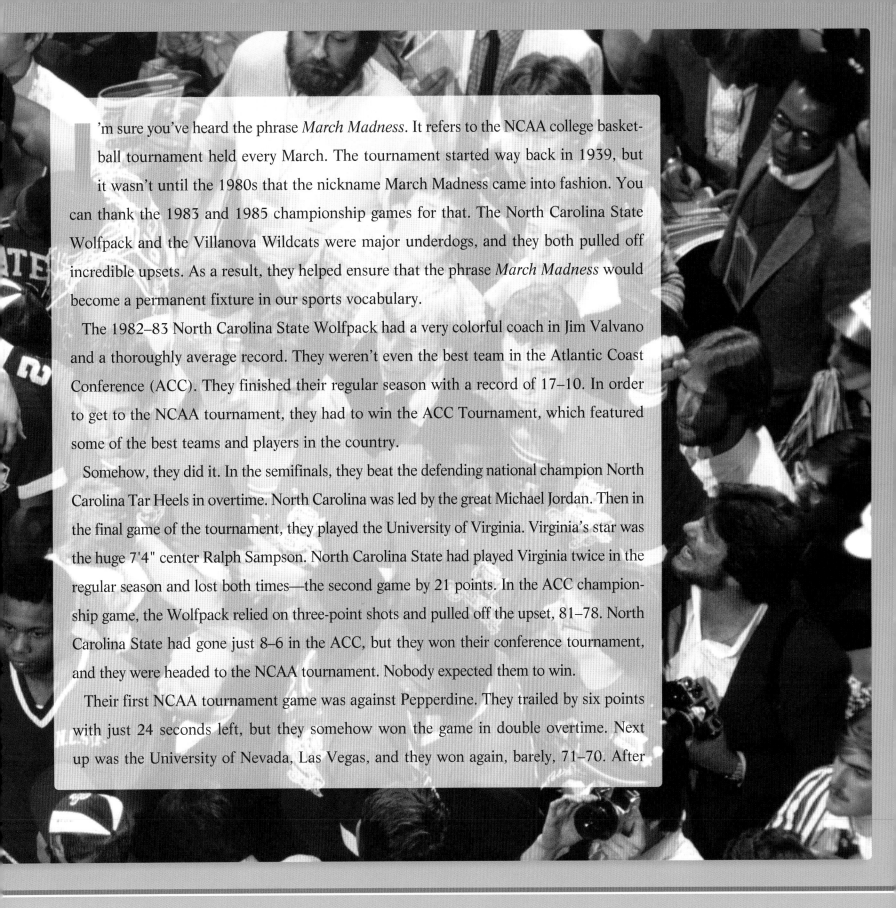

'm sure you've heard the phrase *March Madness*. It refers to the NCAA college basketball tournament held every March. The tournament started way back in 1939, but it wasn't until the 1980s that the nickname March Madness came into fashion. You can thank the 1983 and 1985 championship games for that. The North Carolina State Wolfpack and the Villanova Wildcats were major underdogs, and they both pulled off incredible upsets. As a result, they helped ensure that the phrase *March Madness* would become a permanent fixture in our sports vocabulary.

The 1982–83 North Carolina State Wolfpack had a very colorful coach in Jim Valvano and a thoroughly average record. They weren't even the best team in the Atlantic Coast Conference (ACC). They finished their regular season with a record of 17–10. In order to get to the NCAA tournament, they had to win the ACC Tournament, which featured some of the best teams and players in the country.

Somehow, they did it. In the semifinals, they beat the defending national champion North Carolina Tar Heels in overtime. North Carolina was led by the great Michael Jordan. Then in the final game of the tournament, they played the University of Virginia. Virginia's star was the huge 7'4" center Ralph Sampson. North Carolina State had played Virginia twice in the regular season and lost both times—the second game by 21 points. In the ACC championship game, the Wolfpack relied on three-point shots and pulled off the upset, 81–78. North Carolina State had gone just 8–6 in the ACC, but they won their conference tournament, and they were headed to the NCAA tournament. Nobody expected them to win.

Their first NCAA tournament game was against Pepperdine. They trailed by six points with just 24 seconds left, but they somehow won the game in double overtime. Next up was the University of Nevada, Las Vegas, and they won again, barely, 71–70. After a relatively easy win against the University of Utah, the Wolfpack had to face Virginia for the fourth time that season, with a trip to the Final Four hanging in the balance. Lorenzo Charles for North Carolina State hit two

Thurl Bailey of North Carolina State dunks the ball in the championship game against Houston.

huge foul shots, and the Wolfpack upset Virginia again, 63–62. Remember that name: Lorenzo Charles.

The 1983 Final Four was played in Albuquerque, New Mexico. North Carolina State continued its Cinderella run, beating the University of Georgia 67–60 in the semifinals.

In the other semifinal, Houston took on Louisville. The Houston Cougars, with a wide assortment of colorful dunks, won by 13 points to reach the championship game. It wasn't a surprise. They had lost only twice all season. All their dunking led to a catchy nickname: Phi Slama Jama. And they featured two future Hall of Famers: center Hakeem Olajuwon and the fabulous shooter Clyde "the Glide" Drexler. When the NBA listed the 50 greatest players in NBA history, both of them made it. Now the Cougars would play for the NCAA championship, where they would face a scrappy North Carolina State team. The day of the game, one sportswriter wrote, "Trees will tap dance, elephants will drive in the Indianapolis 500…before North Carolina State finds a way to beat Houston."

Talk about David versus Goliath. Houston arrived at the championship game with a 30–2 record, including 26 straight wins. They hadn't lost a game in nearly four months. North Carolina State showed up after barely surviving several close games. Their record was now 25–10, and no team with as many as 10 losses had ever won the championship.

In those days, the men's college game didn't use a shot clock as it does now, so a team could hold the ball as long as it wanted before shooting. That was a big part of Coach Jim Valvano's strategy. He had it written on the team's blackboard in the locker room. At the last minute, he erased the blackboard. He had a change of heart. He told the team, "If you think we're going to hold the ball in front of 40 million people [watching on TV], you're crazy." He told his team to go out and attack.

In truth, they did both. The Wolfpack played a controlled offense, and on defense, they stopped Houston from all their dunking. At halftime, North Carolina State had a surprising eight-point lead. It wasn't enough. At the start of the second half, Houston dominated, and with 10 minutes remaining, the Cougars opened up their own seven-point lead. But North Carolina State pecked away. The Wolfpack started fouling Houston, and the Cougars missed their free throws. With 1:59 to go in the game, Dereck Whittenburg hit his second-straight shot for the Wolfpack, tying the game at 52. After Houston missed another foul shot, North Carolina State got the ball back and called timeout with just 44 seconds left.

When play resumed, the clock ticked down, but the Wolfpack couldn't find an open shot. Finally, Whittenburg hoisted up a long prayer from way outside. It was an air

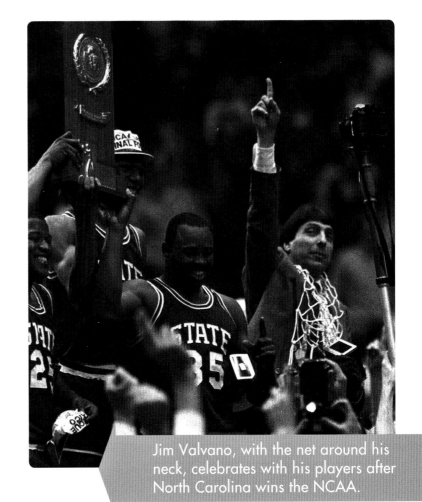

Jim Valvano, with the net around his neck, celebrates with his players after North Carolina wins the NCAA.

ball. But waiting to catch it was Lorenzo Charles. He dunked it home at the buzzer. Pandemonium.

Jim Valvano went racing around the court looking for someone to hug. North Carolina State had done it again. The Wolfpack stunned the basketball world by winning the national championship, 54–52. Trees weren't dancing, and elephants weren't driving race cars, but it was one of the greatest upsets in the history of college basketball.

And then, just two years later, it happened again!

The next season, Houston lost again in the championship

game, this time to the powerful Georgetown Hoyas, who were led by their great center, Patrick Ewing. In 1985 Ewing and company had a chance to win back-to-back championships until a very unlikely opponent came along. The Villanova Wildcats, just like North Carolina State two years earlier, had a very average regular season. They played in the tough Big East Conference along with Georgetown, and during conference play, Villanova had managed a record of just 9–7. Georgetown's conference record was a terrific 14–2. The Hoyas had beaten Villanova both times they had played, but remember—there was no shot clock and both games were low scoring. That was a tip-off of things to come.

In the NCAA tournament, Villanova played a series of close defensive games. They opened the tourney with a two-point win over Dayton and followed that with a four-point win over Michigan. And so it went—all the way to the Final Four in Lexington, Kentucky. In the semifinal game, the Wildcats knocked off Memphis State 52–45. And suddenly, there they were in the championship game. They were one of the unlikeliest finalists of all time, just as North Carolina State had been two years earlier.

Now they had to deal with the Georgetown Hoyas for the third time in less than three months. The Hoyas came into the championship game riding a 16-game winning streak. They had rolled through their regular season. They won the Big East Conference championship at Madison

Villanova's Harold Pressley goes for the basket against Georgetown's Patrick Ewing.

Square Garden, and they weren't really challenged in the NCAA tournament. None of their games were nail-biters, and they had beaten another Big East rival, St. John's, in the semifinal game by 18 points! In short, Georgetown looked unbeatable. They were a sure bet to win their second-straight NCAA basketball championship.

Then they played the game.

Villanova coach Rollie Massimino had a simple message for his team—play to win, don't play not to lose. There's a big difference. He wanted his Wildcats to play with confidence and not be tentative against the more talented Georgetown team.

As the first half unfolded, Georgetown looked to be the better team. The Hoyas built up a quick six-point lead, but Villanova hung around. As the first half was winding down, the Wildcats held on to the ball without shooting for nearly two minutes. Harold Pressley then drove toward the basket, and he scored over Ewing. Villanova had grabbed the halftime lead, 29–28.

Many experts have called Villanova's second half that night *perfect*. It wasn't. The Wildcats missed one shot. That's all. And they still couldn't put the Hoyas away. They built up leads of six points and then five, and both times, Georgetown fought back. With just under five minutes to go, the Hoyas took a one-point lead. It would be their last. Harold Jensen made an open jumper for Villanova from the right side as the Wildcats regained the lead, 55–54. It was their last basket. Georgetown was forced to keep fouling Villanova, and the Wildcats kept making their free throws. When it was over, the

scoreboard read: Villanova 66, Georgetown 64. It was another classic case of David beating Goliath. Instead of using a slingshot, the underdog used a basketball, shooting 78.6 percent from the field. It was an NCAA

Villanova's Ed Pinckney celebrates their win against Georgetown for the national championship in the 1985 NCAA Final Four.

championship game record—nothing short of amazing. Rollie Massimino called it a miracle. Twice in just three years, North Carolina State and Villanova had shocked the basketball world. It was sheer madness.

"I AM THE GREATEST"

Muhammad Ali's journey began in Louisville, Kentucky. His given name was Cassius Clay, and if it weren't for one February night in Miami Beach, Florida, in 1964, you might not be reading this story. But that's exactly what upsets and underdogs are all about. The truth is, if Cassius's bicycle hadn't been stolen when he was 12 years old, he might not have become a boxer. When he told a policeman about the bike, he said he wanted to find the thief who stole it so he could beat him up. It turns out that the policeman was a boxing coach, and he told young Cassius that he better learn how to box. And box he did. That's basically all he did.

Cassius went on to fight 108 amateur bouts, winning the Kentucky Golden Gloves championship six times. He also won two National Golden Gloves tournaments and two National Amateur Athletic Union (AAU) titles all before he was 18 years old. In 1960 he went to Rome, Italy, to represent the United States in the Olympics. He won in the light heavyweight division and brought home the gold medal. When he got back to Louisville, a parade was held in his honor. But there was segregation in some parts of the country, and he was denied service at a local restaurant even though he was a national hero. Legend has it he got so mad that he threw his gold medal into the Ohio River. True or not, he had made a name for himself—and it was just the beginning.

Shortly thereafter, Cassius became a professional boxer. His first match was against a West Virginia police chief named Tunney Hunsaker. Cassius won a six-round decision. Over the next three-and-a-half years, he fought 18 times, winning every fight—most of them by knockout. Cassius was tall—6'3"—and he relied on quick hands and feet. When he later changed his named to Muhammad Ali, he developed the "Ali Shuffle," where he would deliver punches while "dancing" in the ring.

Cassius famously described his own style by saying he would "float like a butterfly, sting like a bee." In fact, he said lots of things. Nowadays, it's called *trash talking* when an athlete brags about how great he is. Cassius may have invented the art of trash talking. He would often proclaim "I am the greatest." Pretty boastful, wouldn't you say? Soon, people everywhere were calling him by his nickname: "the Greatest."

Cassius Clay connects with a left to the face of Sonny Liston.

And he was a clever poet. Before his fights, Cassius would make his predictions in rhyme. For example, he'd boast about an upcoming opponent: "When you come to the fight, don't block the aisles and don't block the door, for you all may go home after round four." And while he

later became a beloved sports figure, his youthful boasting caused many boxing fans to hope that the mouthy braggart would be put in his place.

But he kept on winning. In 1962 he fought former light heavyweight champ Archie Moore. Cassius was 20, and Moore was 47. Cassius predicted that he'd knock Moore out in the fourth round, and that's exactly what he did. The next year, he fought Britain's Henry Cooper in London. In the fourth round, Cooper knocked down Cassius. But Cassius had predicted he would win in five, and again, his prediction proved correct. He was now 18–0 as a pro fighter and was ready for his biggest test. He would face the heavyweight champion of the world: Sonny Liston.

Liston was a menacing figure—and for good reason. As a young man, he had turned to a life of crime and received a five-year sentence in the Missouri State Penitentiary for armed robbery. It was there that he took up the sport of boxing. When he got out of prison, he started his boxing career. He began with a first-round knockout in 1953,

SONNY LISTON VS CASSIUS CLAY JR.

BORN: around 1932

BIRTHPLACE: St. Francis County, AR

HEIGHT: 6'1"

WEIGHT: 215 lbs.

REACH: 84"

LIFETIME RECORD: 50–4

BORN: January 17, 1942

BIRTHPLACE: Louisville, KY

HEIGHT: 6'3"

WEIGHT: 215 lbs.

REACH: 79"

LIFETIME RECORD: 56–5

and over the next 10 years, he won all his fights except one. He was tough, a devastating puncher, but unlike Cassius, he didn't have a colorful personality. He was surly, and he picked up the nickname "the Big Bear."

Liston finally got his title shot in September of 1962. He challenged the heavyweight champion of the world: Floyd Patterson. To show you how feared Liston was, even though he was the challenger, he was the favorite to win the fight. And win it he did. He knocked out Patterson in the first round. It was the first time in history that a challenger had knocked out the heavyweight champ in the first round of a championship fight. And the next year, in the rematch with Patterson, he did it again—another first-round knockout.

Liston was now 35–1 and appeared to be unstoppable. Next up, that brash young kid, Cassius Clay.

The fight was set for Convention Hall in Miami Beach on February 25, 1964. With his tough exterior and impressive record, Sonny Liston was considered the heavy favorite. Few people gave Cassius a chance. But that didn't stop him from shooting off his mouth. He continued with the poems and the insults. For example:

This I predict and I know the score,
I'll be champ of the world in '64.
Here I predict Mr. Liston's dismemberment,
I'll hit him so hard, he'll wonder where
October and November went.

Cassius would taunt Liston whenever he could. He would show up at Liston's training sessions and even at his house, trying to get on his nerves. The morning of the big fight, the traditional weigh-in was held. It was crazy. Cassius continued to yell at Liston, calling him "the Big Ugly Bear." Cassius again made a prediction, proclaiming that Liston "would go down in eight to prove I'm great." Liston didn't say anything. He just held up two fingers as if to indicate that he'd knock out Cassius

Cassius Clay lets loose a barrage of punches against heavyweight champion Sonny Liston.

in the second round. But Cassius had an answer for that too. He said, "Your hands can't hit what your eyes can't see."

It was fight night. You would think that such a big event would draw a huge crowd. It didn't. Because most people expected Sonny Liston to easily beat Cassius Clay, the arena was half empty. On radio, the announcer said it would be a big surprise if the fight lasted longer than one round. After all, Liston had twice beaten Floyd Patterson in the first round.

When it began, Liston was the stalker; Cassius the dancer. Liston would plod after Cassius, and Cassius would keep bounding away. This went on for a couple of minutes—and then Cassius went on the attack. He landed combinations of punches on Liston. When the bell sounded to end the round, the two kept fighting anyway. They had to be separated. Already the fight was a surprise.

Not only had Cassius survived the first round, he was looking terrific. He made it safely through the second round too. So much for Liston's prediction. In the third round, Cassius opened up a cut under Liston's left eye. It wasn't big, and Liston's corner treated it between rounds.

But in the fourth round, Cassius was the one who had trouble seeing. Something had gotten into his eyes. After the round, Cassius said he couldn't see, but his trainer washed out his eyes and sent out his fighter for the fifth round. That's when Liston went on the attack. He sensed that Cassius was in trouble, and he tried to end it right then and there. Cassius kept protecting his head with his gloves and continued to dance away. Liston stalked him, but it was no use. Cassius not only survived his eye problems, but he had also survived the fifth round. Now Liston was clearly in unfamiliar territory. Only one of his fights in the last four years had gone this long.

In the sixth round, Cassius went on the attack, throwing lefts and rights at the champion. Now the roles had reversed. Cassius was the stalker, and it was Liston who was backing up. The sixth round ended uneventfully. But then something unbelievable happened. When the bell sounded for the start of the seventh round, Liston just sat there on his stool. He

refused to continue. The fight was over! Cassius had done the unimaginable: he had defeated the "unbeatable" Sonny Liston.

Cassius danced to the middle of the ring and threw up his arms in victory. He was now the heavyweight champion of the world, and he was mobbed. And then his mouth

Cassius Clay celebrates with a cake depicting himself and the defeated Sonny Liston.

went into overdrive. He had predicted that he'd win in eight, so he said of Liston, "He wanted to go to heaven, so I took him in seven." Cassius kept repeating "I'm king of the world...I shook up the world." And, of course, over and over, he proclaimed, "I am the greatest."

For the first time, nobody could argue.

"THE GIANTS WIN THE PENNANT"

There have been more than a quarter-of-a-million home runs hit in the history of Major League Baseball. Out of all those homers, can you call one the greatest? The one I would vote for was hit at the Polo Grounds on October 3, 1951. It's known as "the Shot Heard 'round the World." It was accompanied by perhaps the most famous play-by-play call of all time. But the dramatic home run and the historic call amount to the icing on the cake. Let me start at the beginning.

In 1951 things were very different in baseball. There were eight teams in the American League and eight more in the National. Only the team that finished first in each league would go to the World Series. There were no playoffs and no wild cards. Of the 16 teams in Major League Baseball at the time, three of them were in New York City. The Yankees played in the Bronx, the Dodgers in Brooklyn, and the New York Giants in Manhattan—on a piece of land called Coogan's Bluff. That's where the Polo Grounds stood. The Giants and Dodgers were in the National League, and because they shared the same city, they were bitter rivals.

On August 11 in Philadelphia, future Hall of Famer Robin Roberts pitched a shutout for the Phillies against the Giants. That same day in Brooklyn, Duke Snider hit a first-inning homer as the Dodgers cruised to an 8–1 win over the Boston Braves in the first game of a doubleheader. At that moment, here's what the National League standings looked like:

TEAM	WINS	LOSSES	GAMES BEHIND
Brooklyn	70	35	—
New York	59	51	13½

The second-place New York Giants trailed the Brooklyn Dodgers by a whopping 13½ games, and the Giants had only 44 games left to catch them. No team had ever been so far out of first place in August and managed to win the pennant.

After getting shut out by the Phillies, the Giants played Philadelphia three more times and won them all. Next up, the first-place Dodgers at the Polo Grounds. After the Giants won the first game of the series, the second game was tied 1–1 in the top of the eighth. Brooklyn had a runner on third when Carl Furillo launched a shot into the gap in right-center. The Giants rookie center fielder, Willie Mays, had been playing the right-handed Furillo over in left-center, so Mays had a lot of ground to make up. The speedy Mays made a lunging catch, but what followed stunned everyone. Billy Cox tagged up at third base, trying to score the lead run. Mays spun completely around and fired the ball home. It was a perfect throw to nail Cox and keep the score tied.

In the bottom of the eighth, Mays singled off Dodgers pitcher Ralph Branca. Remember that name. Mays wound up scoring the winning run as the Giants won 3–1. Brooklyn's lead was now down to 10½ games. The comeback was under way.

Between August 12 and August 27, the Giants played 16 games and won them all. What was an insurmountable 13½ game deficit was suddenly sliced to five games.

With one week to go in the season, the Giants still trailed by four. They didn't lose another game, sweeping

New York Giants outfielder Willie Mays

Hank Bauer of the Yankees takes a swing in the 1951 World Series.

The scene shifted to the Polo Grounds for the second game. The great Jackie Robinson hit a two-run homer for the Dodgers in the top of the first, and Brooklyn was off and running. They bombed the Giants with four homers and easily won Game 2 of the play-off, 10–0. That set the stage for a dramatic third game—just one game to decide which team would go the World Series. It

their final seven. The Dodgers lost four games and—*bingo!* The two teams finished the season tied for first place. There would be a three-game playoff between the two rivals to decide the National League pennant.

The first game was played at Ebbets Field in Brooklyn. The Dodgers held a 1–0 lead when Bobby Thomson for the Giants hit a two-run homer off Ralph Branca. Remember both of those names. The Giants went on to win the game 3–1. Just one more win and the team that had been 13½ games out of first place only seven weeks earlier would win the pennant.

was a battle of aces that day at the Polo Grounds. The Dodgers had their best pitcher on the mound in Don Newcombe. Newk had won 20 games that season. The Giants countered with their best, Sal Maglie. He had won 23 games. As expected, the game turned out to be a tight one. In the top of the first, the Dodgers drew first blood. Jackie Robinson singled to left, scoring Pee Wee Reese. It was 1–0 Brooklyn.

That's where things stood until the bottom of the seventh inning. The Giants Bobby Thomson then hit a sacrifice fly, bringing home Monte Irvin with the tying run. After seven innings of play, it was a nail-biter, 1–1. Then Brooklyn broke things open in the eighth. Thanks to four singles and a wild pitch from Maglie, the Dodgers exploded for three runs. It was now 4–1 Brooklyn, and it stayed that way heading to the bottom of the ninth. A three-run Dodgers lead

Bobby Thomson of the New York Giants hits a home run to win the National League pennant.

LISTEN to this MOMENT TRACK 5

looked just as insurmountable as their 13½ game lead had looked back in August.

Don Newcombe went out to the mound to start the ninth for Brooklyn. Alvin Dark was the leadoff hitter for the Giants, and he legged out an infield hit. The next batter was Don Mueller. He lined the first pitch to right for another single, and just like that, the Giants had the potential tying run coming up with nobody out. Monte Irvin was the batter, and he hit a pop-up that was caught in foul territory for the first out. Just two outs to go and the Dodgers would win the pennant. Whitey Lockman was the next batter for New York, and he doubled down the left-field line. Dark raced home, Mueller scampered to third, and it was now 4–2 Dodgers, second and third, one out, as Bobby Thomson strolled to the plate.

Dodgers manager Charlie Dressen then made a pitching change. He was taking Newcombe out and replacing him with Ralph Branca. Remember, Branca had been on the mound in Game 1 when Thomson hit a two-run homer. First base was open. Willie Mays was standing in the on-deck circle. Would the Dodgers intentionally walk Thomson to set up a force at any base? No. They would pitch to Bobby Thomson.

Thomson would later say that his thoughts were very simple as he walked to the plate. He told himself, "Wait and watch. Give yourself a chance to hit." He waited and watched the first pitch from Branca. It was a fastball right down the middle. Strike one.

It was a Wednesday afternoon at 3:58 p.m. Branca was about to throw his second pitch to Thomson. Up in the radio booth, Russ Hodges was the Giants announcer. Here's how he described what happened next:

Branca throws. There's a long drive. It's gonna be, I believe—the Giants win the pennant! The Giants win the pennant! The Giants win the pennant! The Giants win the pennant! Bobby Thomson hits into the lower deck of the left-field stands. The Giants win the pennant, and they're going crazy! They're going crazy!

Yup, they were certainly going crazy at the Polo Grounds that day. The 34,320 fans had witnessed what I consider to be the greatest home run in baseball history. It was a three-run, pennant-clinching homer that enabled

The New York Giants converge on Bobby Thompson after his pennant-winning home run.

the New York Giants to beat the rival Brooklyn Dodgers 5–4 and complete an unbelievable comeback to win the National League pennant. Bobby Thomson skipped around the bases, and when he got to home plate, he was mobbed by his Giants teammates. They lifted him onto their shoulders and carried him off the field. Russ Hodges kept announcing:

"I don't believe it. I don't believe it. I do not believe it."

Few fans could. And that's why to this day, they call it "the Miracle of Coogan's Bluff."

BILLY WHO?

When it comes to the Olympics, the United States has won more gold medals than any other country. Many of the winners are famous. In track and field, Carl Lewis won nine gold medals at four different Olympics. In swimming, Michael Phelps won eight golds at the Beijing Olympics in 2008 after winning six at the 2004 Olympics in Athens. The United States has also dominated in Olympic basketball. In 1992 the United States won the gold medal in Barcelona with the "Dream Team," which featured some of the greatest basketball players in history all on the same team—players like Michael Jordan, Magic Johnson, and Larry Bird. But there are plenty of Olympic events and athletes that you've probably never heard of. This story is about an American who won an Olympic gold medal in the 10,000 meters. How rare is that? It had never happened before. And it hasn't happened since.

Billy Mills was a Sioux Indian who grew up on a reservation in South Dakota. He had a difficult childhood, with his mother dying when he was just seven. His dad died five years later, so at age 12, young Billy was an orphan being raised by his grandmother. Before he died, Billy's father told him, "Son, you have broken wings, but someday you will have wings like an eagle." What his father meant was that Billy was hurting inside because his mother was no longer alive.

His dad advised Billy to pursue a dream, and by doing so, it would "heal" him. Billy decided to seek that dream in sports. Because his father had been a boxer, Billy boxed too. He also tried football. But what he really liked most was to run, so he decided to dedicate himself to the sport of track. He became so good in high school that he was offered a full track and field scholarship to the University of Kansas.

When Billy went to college, it was the first time he had left his reservation. It wasn't

BILLY MILLS

BORN: June 30, 1938

BIRTHPLACE: Pine Ridge, South Dakota

HEIGHT: 5'11"

WEIGHT: 150 lbs.

UPSETS AND UNDERDOGS

CAREER HIGHLIGHTS: Only American ever to win Olympic Gold in the 10,000 meter run in 1964; was inducted into the U.S. Olympic Hall of Fame in 1984

Billy Mills (No. 722) and the rest of the competitors at the start of the men's 10,000 meter race.

easy for him. He felt alone and discriminated against because he was Native American. He turned his full attention to track and continued to improve. He excelled at cross-country running and was named an All-American, which meant he was one of the best collegians in the country. But the discrimination continued. Billy said there were times during group photo shoots of the runners when he would be asked to step out of the picture. He figured it was because he was the only runner with dark skin. It really bothered him. After one such incident, he was very depressed, but he thought of his father and how he had advised Billy to pursue his dream to "heal" himself. It was then and there that Billy wrote down in a journal, "Gold medal 10,000 meters. Believe, believe, believe." And that was the goal he set for himself.

After college, he joined the Marines, and he increased his training regimen, running 100 miles a week. He was preparing for the Olympic trials in Los Angeles to attempt to qualify for the 1964 U.S. Olympic team. At the trials, in the L.A. Coliseum, Mills finished eight seconds behind the winner, Gerry Lindgren. It was good enough for second place. The top three finishers were heading to Tokyo, Japan, for the 1964 summer games.

Billy wasn't even the best 10,000-meter runner in his own country, but he was going to the Olympics to compete against the greatest 10,000-meter runners in the world. He had overcome many obstacles to get to this point in his life, and the year before the Olympics, he had to face another. Doctors discovered that he was diabetic, meaning he had low blood sugar. The condition saps a person's energy, which of course isn't good for a long-distance runner. It was just one more hurdle that Billy had to clear. On top of that, only one Native American had ever won an Olympic gold medal, and that was the great Jim Thorpe, who won two golds in track and field more than 50 years earlier. Billy's chances of winning appeared slim at best.

On October 14, 1964, 75,000 fans packed the stands to witness 38 runners approach the starting line at Tokyo's National Stadium in Japan. They represented more than 20 countries. What a collection of runners! Ron Clarke from Australia was the world-record holder. Pyotr Bolotnikov of the Soviet Union had won the gold medal four years earlier at the Rome Olympics. Murray Halberg of New Zealand was the 5,000-meter champ in Rome. Mohammed Gammoudi of Tunisia would go on to win the gold medal in the 5,000 meters four years later in Mexico City, Mexico. And Mamo Wolde of Ethiopia would become the 1968 Mexico City Olympic marathon champion. If one nation wasn't expected to compete for a medal, it was the United States. After all, no American had ever won the 10,000 at the Olympics. And at these games, the top U.S. runner, Gerry Lindgren, was running on a sprained ankle. As for Billy Mills? Nobody gave him a second thought.

The gun sounded, and the race was under way—25 laps around the 400-meter track. The early leader was Ron Clarke, the record holder. He was setting a fast pace. As for Mills, early in the race, he said he felt that his blood sugar was low, so he needed to conserve his energy. His plan was to let the

Billy Mills pulls ahead of Mohammed Gammoudi of Tunisia in the 10,000 meter race.

LISTEN to this MOMENT TRACK 6

10,000 METERS is roughly **6.2 MILES**.

other runners go ahead and then try to make one last push at the end of the race. Halfway through the race, there were just five contenders for the lead: Ron Clarke, Mohammed Gammoudi, Mamo Wolde, home country favorite Kokichi Tsuburaya, and surprisingly, Billy Mills. A short while later, the number was down to just four as Tsuburaya faded. But Mills was still there.

It all came down to one final lap, with three runners all jostling for position. Clarke surged to the lead and then Gammoudi did. Back and forth they went, with Mills in third place. Remember, he was conserving his energy for one final kick—and that kick began with only about 100 meters to go. Mills began to charge. He got past Clarke, and only Gammoudi was ahead of him. He had already been running for more than 6 miles, but Billy kept running faster. The TV announcers couldn't believe it. One of them was screaming, "Look at Mills! Look at Mills!" At the very last moment, Mills blasted past Gammoudi and hit the tape. It seemed as if he indeed had "wings like an eagle." Amazingly, he had won. He accomplished the dream goal that he had written down—to "Believe, believe, believe."

How incredible was it? Mills never ran so well in his life. The fastest he had ever run 10,000 meters was more than 29 minutes at the Olympic trials. But on this day, he smashed his personal best by a full 46 seconds. In track and field, that is huge. His winning time was 28 minutes, 24.4 seconds. It was a new Olympic record. He had beaten Gammoudi by just .4 seconds. After he crossed the finish line, one of the Japanese officials grabbed Billy and asked, "Who are you?"

Maybe Ron Clarke summed it up best. He had been favored to win the race, and afterward, he was asked if he had been concerned about Mills. Clarke replied, "Worried about him? I never heard of him."

Now that's what you call an upset.

Billy Mills waves to the crowd after winning the gold medal.

WHAT HAPPENED OFF THE AIR

n 1955 sports coverage on television was very different from the way it is today. Nowadays, when it comes to major golf events, TV networks will stay on the air for hours. But that wasn't the case back then. NBC televised the U.S. Open golf tournament at the Olympic Club in San Francisco, California. For the final round, the network stayed on the air for one whole hour. That was it. Just 60 minutes of golf coverage. As the hour came to a close, the greatest golfer of his era, Ben Hogan, sank a par putt. He was the leader by 1 stroke. He walked off the green and flipped his winning golf ball to an official so that it would go into a golf museum. On the air, NBC congratulated Hogan for winning the U.S. Open. It was his record fifth U.S. Open title. Except for the fact that it wasn't. There was still a golfer out on the course by the name of Jack Fleck. What happened after NBC went off the air started the ball rolling toward perhaps the greatest upset in the history of golf.

JACK FLECK

BORN: November 7, 1921

BIRTHPLACE: Bettendorf, IA

HEIGHT: 6'1"

PLAYS: Right-handed

WEIGHT: 167 lbs.

TURNED PRO: 1939

UPSETS AND UNDERDOGS

CAREER HIGHLIGHT: Won the 1955 U.S. Open

Jack Fleck takes a practice swing before facing off against Ben Hogan for the National Open title.

Any discussion of the greatest golfers includes Ben Hogan. He was said to be the best pure ball striker of all time. He spent hours upon hours practicing golf. While playing, his concentration level was intense. He didn't have a lot of friends—golf was his life. Just 16 months after a horrific car accident in 1949, he won the U.S. Open. The next year, he won it again. It was his fourth U.S. Open championship. In 1953 at age 41, he entered six tournaments. He won five of them, including three majors: the U.S. Open, The Masters, and the British Open. So it wasn't surprising when NBC thought he was the U.S. Open winner that day in 1955 when he walked off the green after completing the 72nd hole.

The great Sam Snead was 5 shots back, and the leading money winner on the golf tour that year, Julius Boros, was 8 shots behind. But Jack Fleck was only one shot back with 4 holes to play. Nobody really knew much about Jack Fleck. But if anyone did, they certainly didn't think he was going to challenge the great Ben Hogan.

On the 15th hole, Jack had a bogey that dropped him 2 shots behind Hogan with just 3 holes to play. But he birdied the 16th and made par on 17, so going to the 18th and final hole, he knew he needed a birdie to tie Hogan and force a playoff. On that fateful 18th hole, he hit his 3 wood off the tee. For his second shot, he took out his 7 iron and hit the ball perfectly onto the green. He was left with an 8-foot putt for the tying birdie. He nailed it! Jack had never won a professional golf tournament. His best finish at a U.S. Open was tied for 52nd place! But he had tied one of the greatest golfers who ever lived—and the next day, he would face him in an 18-hole playoff.

So who exactly was Jack Fleck, and where did he come from? Jack was from Iowa, and like Hogan, he began as a caddy. He was an assistant golf pro before going off to fight in World War II. After the war, he tried to make golf his career. The prize money was minuscule when compared with what pro golfers can win today. Jack had played in 41 tournaments before that 1955 U.S. Open, and he had made a grand total of $7,500. By comparison, the winner of the U.S. Open these days makes way over $1 million for that one tournament. Anyway, in 1955, Fleck came out of nowhere. In one of his practice rounds before the U.S. Open, he shot an 87. That's a terrible score for a golf pro. After the first round of the U.S. Open, he was 9 shots off the lead. Nobody before or after Jack had been that many shots behind after the first round and had gone on to win the championship.

It was June 19, 1955. Jack remembers it as an overcast, damp day in Northern California. He was going head-to-head in an 18-hole playoff with the one and only Ben Hogan to decide the U.S. Open Championship. Most experts just assumed Hogan would be the easy winner. It was truly considered to be David versus Goliath. But in this case, "David's" weapon was a putter.

By his own admission, Fleck wasn't a great putter.

Maybe he wasn't in general, but that day, he was terrific, especially during a five-hole stretch. Here's how the match unfolded. On the 3rd hole, just as Hogan was about to tee off, a rabbit ran onto the tee area and interrupted his concentration. He still hit a great shot but then missed a short birdie putt. Was it an omen? Jack

GOLF TERMS EVERY FAN SHOULD KNOW!

par = standard score for a hole

birdie = a hole played in one stroke under par

eagle = a hole played in two strokes under par

albatross = a hole played three strokes under par, also called a double eagle

bogey = one stroke over par

Ben Hogan congratulates Jack Fleck at the end of the U.S. Open.

Fleck was not only holding his own against the great Ben Hogan, but he was leading by 1 shot after 5 holes.

Golf fans kept waiting for Jack to crack, and on the 6th hole, it looked like he might. He hooked his approach shot into a sand trap, and when he blasted out of the sand, he was still off the green about 20 feet away from the flag. But he holed a long tough putt to avoid a bogey. The 8th hole was a par-3, and Hogan rolled in a 35-footer for a birdie 2. No problem for Jack. He made his putt from around 7 feet to match Hogan's birdie.

Jack kept on making putts. On the next hole, he made a 20-footer for another birdie. And then another one—three birdies in a row. After 10 holes, Jack Fleck was shocking the golf world. He had a 3-stroke lead—but Hogan wasn't about to quit. He birdied 14, and Jack's lead was now down to 2. At 17, Jack made a rare mistake. He missed a short par putt and made bogey. The lead was sliced to just 1. One hole to go for the U.S. Open Championship.

Jack felt that his real strength as a golfer was that he could drive the ball straight off the tee. And that's exactly what he did on the final hole. As for Hogan? He slipped during his swing and hit a terrible shot into thick rough. The ball was buried so deep it took him 3 more shots to get it back into the fairway. Once on the green, he made a very long putt. But he had scored a double bogey 6. Jack made a simple par-4. The improbable had happened. The huge underdog had beaten the legendary Ben Hogan by 3 shots to win the U.S. Open.

For Jack, it was his biggest pay day: $6,000. As a result of his amazing win, he got to meet the president of the United States. He was also invited to go on television shows to talk about his accomplishment.

This time, the correct golfer was congratulated for winning the U.S. Open.

Jack Fleck poses with his championship trophy after defeating Ben Hogan.

JIM ABBOTT

On September 4, 1993, a cloudy Saturday in the Bronx, New York, Yankees pitcher Jim Abbott toed the pitching rubber. It was the top of the ninth inning. A Yankee Stadium crowd of more than 27,000 was on its feet. Kenny Lofton led off for the Cleveland Indians, and he hit a ground ball to second base. That was the first out. The next batter, Felix Fermin, hit a long fly ball that was tracked down in deep left-center field by Bernie Williams. Two outs. Jim Abbott was now just one out away

NO-HITTERS IN YANKEE HISTORY		
NAME	OPPONENT	DATE
Dwight Gooden	Seattle	5/14/1996
Jim Abbott	Cleveland	9/4/1993
Dave Righetti	Boston	7/4/1983
Allie Reynolds	Boston	9/28/1951
Allie Reynolds	Cleveland	7/12/1951
Monte Pearson	Cleveland	8/27/1928
Sad Sam Jones	Philadelphia	9/4/1923
George Mogridge	Boston	4/24/1917

Jim Abbott celebrates his no-hit victory over the Cleveland Indians alongside teammate Wade Boggs.

from pitching a no-hitter. Pretty remarkable when you consider that he was born without a right hand.

Jim grew up in Flint, Michigan, and he loved sports. Because he didn't have a right hand, his parents tried to interest him in playing soccer. But all his friends were playing baseball, and that's what Jim wanted to do. He practiced for hours. He would work on pitching the ball and shifting his glove back and forth so he could catch a ball in his glove and then tuck the glove under his right arm, grabbing the ball out of the glove and throwing it to first—all in one motion! He learned to do it quickly and effortlessly. He was now ready to play Little League baseball.

In Jim's very first game, he threw a no-hitter. Amazing. And that was just the beginning. At Flint Central High School, he not only pitched, but he played first base and outfield. Yup, he could play in the field. Not only that, he could also hit. He didn't have two hands on the bat, but that didn't stop him. In his senior year, he led the team in pitching *and* hitting. While batting .427, he pitched four no-hitters.

The high school football coach took notice of his strong left arm and insisted Jim play on the football team, even though he had never played football. He not only played quarterback, but he also proved to have a pretty good leg serving as the team's punter. In Jim's mind, not having a hand didn't make him different—it just meant he had to learn to do things differently. And he learned to do them just as well as people with two hands. At every level of competition, there were those who doubted he could take the next step, and he kept proving them all wrong.

After high school, Jim was drafted to play in the major leagues by the Toronto Blue Jays. He turned them down and went to the University of Michigan. He continued to excel on the diamond, and the awards piled up. In 1988 he was voted the best college baseball player in the nation, and he also won the award as the best male athlete in the Big Ten Conference. No baseball player had ever won that award before. He capped off the year by pitching for the U.S. Olympic baseball team at the 1988 Summer Games in Seoul, South Korea. He was on the mound when the United States beat Japan 5–3. You could now add Olympic gold medal winner to his growing list of accomplishments.

After the Olympics, Jim was again drafted to play Major League Baseball, this time by the California Angels. He was the eighth pick in the first round. That's how much the Angels thought of his ability, not to mention his 95 mph fastball. Most people thought he would have to spend time in the minor leagues working on his fielding. But as usual, Jim surprised the doubters. He pitched well enough in spring training to make the Opening Day roster. Jim Abbott had made it to the major leagues straight out of high school without a right hand and without pitching a day in the minors.

On April 8, 1989, Jim made his major league debut in Anaheim against the Seattle Mariners. It was a World Series atmosphere. Nearly 48,000 fans came out to see him pitch, which was more than double the size of the previous night's crowd. Before the game, he even received a congratulatory telegram from his boyhood idol, Nolan Ryan.

Jim Abbott gets ready to release a pitch.

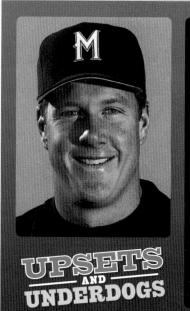

JIM ABBOTT

BORN: September 19, 1967

BIRTHPLACE: Flint, MI

HEIGHT: 6'3"

WEIGHT: 200 lbs.

TEAMS: California Angels, New York Yankees, Chicago White Sox, Milwaukee Brewers

POSITION: Pitcher

ROOKIE YEAR: 1989

CAREER ERA: 4.25

UPSETS AND UNDERDOGS

Jim Abbott steps up to bat.

Jim pitched into the fifth inning, giving up six singles and three earned runs. When he left the game, he received a standing ovation from the crowd. But the Angels lost the game 7–0, and Jim was the losing pitcher. A couple of weeks later, in his third start, he pitched six strong innings and got his first major league win against the Baltimore Orioles. He finished his rookie season with a 12–12 record. Not bad. When they voted for Rookie of the Year, he earned fifth place.

Two years later, in 1991, he had his finest season. He won 18 games for the Angels and had the best earned run average (ERA) of any of the starting pitchers on his team. That season, Roger Clemens of the Boston Red Sox won his third Cy Young Award as the American League's top pitcher. Jim Abbott came in third. By then, more and more people no longer thought of him as a "one-armed pitcher." He was now considered just a "pitcher"—and a good one at that.

His last year in the major leagues was 1999, when he pitched for the Milwaukee Brewers. It was his first time in the National League. There is no designated hitter in the National League as there is in the American, which meant Jim now had to bat. In a June game against the Cubs, essentially holding the bat with one hand, Jim singled and drove home a run. He was in his 10th season, and it was his first major league hit and run batted in. Jim Abbott had now truly done it all on a major league baseball diamond.

Let's go back to Yankee Stadium for that September Saturday afternoon in 1993. Jim Abbott needed one more out for his no-hitter. Carlos Baerga was at the plate for the Indians. He hit a groundball to the left side, where shortstop Randy Velarde fielded it and threw to first baseman Don Mattingly for the final out of the game. On television, the announcer was yelling:

He did it! He did it!
No-hitter for Jim Abbott.
Jim Abbott throws a no-hitter.
He's mobbed by his teammates!

It was a remarkable accomplishment, especially when you consider what had happened earlier that week. The previous Sunday, against the same Cleveland team, Jim pitched one of the worst games of the year. He had given up 10 hits and seven runs in less than four innings. Jim said, "You might be down now, but you don't know what's going to happen tomorrow." Six days later, he rebounded to pitch just the

eighth no-hitter in the long and glorious history of the New York Yankees—with only one hand, no less. No big deal. He had been bouncing back and exceeding expectations all his life.

Jim Abbott and the U.S. team celebrate a gold medal win against Japan in the 1988 Olympics.

THE MAGNIFICENT SEVEN

In the 1996 Centennial Summer Olympics, the U.S. women's gymnastics team takes home gold. From left are Amanda Borden, Dominique Dawes, Amy Chow, Jaycie Phelps, Dominique Moceanu, Kerri Strug, and Shannon Miller.

Winners come in all shapes and sizes. The "biggest" winner in this book weighed more than 1,000 pounds—the racehorse named Upset. On the other end of the spectrum is a pint-sized gymnast who weighed in at a mere 75 pounds. This is the story of how she and her teammates accomplished something that had never been done before.

When it comes to women's gymnastics, no team has dominated like the Soviet Union. Their women won the Olympic team gold medal for the first time in 1952, and they kept on winning it Olympics after Olympics. Between 1952 and 1992, women from the Soviet Union won every single gold medal except for one—in 1984. They might have won that one too, but they didn't show up. The Soviet Union boycotted the Los Angeles Olympics.

The 1996 Olympics were staged in Atlanta, Georgia. Seven young women comprised the U.S. women's gymnastics team. They would try to make history by capturing the first ever U.S. women's Olympic team gold medal. They were nicknamed "the Magnificent Seven": Amanda Borden, Amy Chow, Dominique Dawes, Shannon Miller, Dominique Moceanu, Jaycie Phelps, and Kerri Strug. They ranged in age from 14 to 19 years old. Dominique Moceanu trained in Houston, Texas. At 14, she was the youngest member of the team. She was also the tiniest at just 4'7" and 75 pounds. There was one other member of the team who was under 5 feet tall: Kerri Strug from Tucson, Arizona. She stood 4'8", but before the 1996 Olympics were over, her stature would grow to enormous proportions.

Coming into the 1996 games, the Romanian women were the favorites to win the team gold. They were the two-time reigning world champs. The Russian and Chinese were also strong. As for the Americans, they had won the team bronze medal at the 1995 World Championships, and they were expected to compete for a medal, but they

KERRI STRUG

BORN: November 19, 1977

BIRTHPLACE: Tucson, AZ

HEIGHT: 4'8"

WEIGHT: 82 lbs.

TEAM: U.S. Olympic Gymnastics Team

SPECIALTIES: Uneven bars and floor exercises

FAST FACT: She was the youngest Olympian at the 1992 Olympics in Barcelona at age 14.

UPSETS AND UNDERDOGS

CAREER HIGHLIGHTS: Won the Olympic Bronze in 1992 and Olympic Gold in 1996

There are two parts to the team competition: the compulsories and the optionals. Each counts for 50 percent of the total score. When all the teams had completed their compulsory routines, the U.S. women were ahead of the world champion Romanians, but they trailed the surprising Russians. Two days later, they would all compete for gold.

The date was July 23, 1996. The venue was the Georgia Dome, home to the Olympic gymnastics competition. It was time for the optionals, and the American girls were more than ready—they put on a spectacular show. Jaycie Phillips started it off on the uneven parallel bars. A 16-year-old from Greenfield, Indiana, Jaycie performed nearly flawlessly. Fans were chanting "U-S-A, U-S-A." Those chants would only grow louder. One by one, the Magnificent Seven mounted the uneven bars, and each one was nearly perfect. Last to go was Dominique Dawes from Silver Spring, Maryland, and her score was the best of all: 9.850. The United States had now taken the lead for the gold medal, but there were still three more exercises to go.

The Magnificent Seven continued to perform magnificently. Next were the floor exercises, in which Dominique Dawes matched her 9.850 from the unevens. Again, she had the top American score. Then they competed on the balance beam, where Shannon Miller led the way. There

were hardly the favorites. A couple of the girls were nursing injuries. Dominique Moceanu had a stress fracture in her tibia (shinbone), and Shannon Miller had tendonitis in her wrist. Both of them were unable to compete at the U.S. Olympic trials but were named to the team based on how they had done at other tournaments. When the girls got to Atlanta, they didn't live in the athletes' village as most Olympians do. They stayed at a private location to avoid distractions. As a result, they bonded as a team.

LISTEN to this MOMENT TRACK 7

was just one rotation left—the vault—and the Americans now had a commanding first-place lead over the Russians.

Each girl had to vault twice. As long as there weren't any disasters, it would be the Americans climbing the podium to claim the gold medals. But then suddenly, for the first time, they ran into trouble. The tiniest gymnast, Dominique Moceanu, fell on both of her vault attempts. Her score was just 9.2—far below all the other scores. It all came down to Kerri Strug, who wasn't the most well known in the group.

Kerri was 18 years old, and it seemed as if she had been involved in gymnastics for her entire life. She was doing flips and somersaults from the time she was four. When she was eight, she entered gymnastics competitions, and as she started winning local and regional events, she wanted more. She was 12 years old when she decided she wanted to compete in the Olympics. She realized she needed a great coach, so when she was 13 she moved away from home in Tucson, Arizona, to train with world-famous gymnastics coach Bela Karolyi in Houston.

Karolyi had been the coach for Nadia Comeneci when the 14-year-old Romanian girl stunned the gymnastics world. She was the first in Olympics history to score a perfect 10 back in Montreal in 1976. In 1991

Shannon Miller performs her balance beam routine in the 1996 Olympic Games.

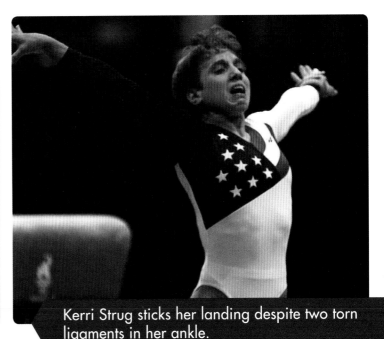

Kerri Strug sticks her landing despite two torn ligaments in her ankle.

coached by Karolyi, Kerri won the vault at the U.S. Gymnastics Championships. At age 13, she was on her way. As a 14-year-old, she made the U.S. Olympic team and helped them win a bronze medal in Barcelona, Spain, in 1992.

Now it was all up to her in Atlanta. Could the U.S. women finally win their first-ever team gold in Olympic gymnastics? Kerri came running toward the vault, did a handspring, and twisted through the air for her dismount. And then it happened. She slipped on her landing and fell backward. She heard a snap in her ankle. Something was terribly wrong. Her score didn't make her feel any better: 9.162. Suddenly the girls were losing their grip on the gold medal. But Kerri had one more chance. She had to jump again within 30 seconds, but she couldn't feel her leg. Would she be able to do it? If she didn't vault, her 9.162 would be her final score, and the Russians might win the gold. She didn't know it at the time, but she had torn two ligaments in her left ankle. She thought to herself, "This is what you dream about from when you're five years old." She wasn't going to quit now.

So on her bad ankle, she sprinted toward the vault a second time. She did her handspring and had to land on both feet, throbbing ankle and all. And she did it! She stuck her landing and didn't fall. With pain shooting up her leg, she somehow managed to stand upright.

Kerri Strug is carried by her coach, Bela Karolyi, to receive the gold medal.

The crowd went wild. She immediately starting hopping around on one leg before falling to the mat. Then her score went up: 9.712. The U.S. team had won the gold!

Kerri Strug couldn't walk on her own. She had to go to the hospital to get checked out. But at that moment, the hospital could wait. She wanted to be with her teammates. Bela Karolyi picked her up and carried her to the podium to receive her gold medal. It was a touching moment. As the gold medal was placed around her neck, the crowd again chanted "U-S-A, U-S-A!" It was bittersweet for Kerri. The ankle injury prevented her from competing in the individual competition, but because of her courage, Kerri helped her team make history. It was truly magnificent.

THE BAND OF NO-HOPERS

The World Cup is considered to be the biggest sports event in the world. It comes around every four years and pits country against country in soccer. In the United States, soccer continues to grow as millions of kids play it. But back in 1950, it was a different story. Soccer wasn't nearly as popular in the United States as it is now. So when the United States qualified to play in the World Cup in Brazil, there wasn't a whole lot of interest. The games weren't even on television. When the U.S. team went to South America to compete in the tournament, only one American sportswriter covered the event, and his newspaper didn't even pay for his trip—he had to travel on his own. Nobody thought the U.S. team would do very well—in fact, it was given virtually no chance at all. The odds of the United States winning the tournament were 500–1. For the Americans' first match, they played Spain. The United States took a 1–0 lead but couldn't hold it. As expected, Spain won 3–1.

On July 29, 1950, the U.S. team played its second match against mighty England. England had invented the sport of soccer in the 1800s and the experts all predicted that the English would win the 1950 World Cup. As for their American opponents, a newspaper in Ireland called the U.S. soccer team a "band of no-hopers." Talk about underdogs! And it's easy to understand why everyone felt that way.

To begin with, the coach of the American team, Bill Jeffrey, was given the job less than two weeks before the World Cup began. Jeffrey was the soccer coach at Penn State University, and he had to quickly assemble a team. They were mostly part-time soccer players—many of them from St. Louis, Missouri. They all had other jobs. For example, the goaltender, Frank Borghi, drove a hearse for his uncle's funeral home. He grew up in the same St. Louis neighborhood as a couple of kids who went on to become famous baseball players: Yogi Berra and Joe Garagiola. But Frank preferred to play soccer.

The captain of the team, Walter Bahr, was a high school gym teacher from Philadelphia. Joe Gaetjens was originally from Haiti. He was studying accounting at Columbia University in New York City and to earn an income, he washed dishes in a restaurant. One player couldn't play for the U.S. team because his boss wouldn't give him the time off from work. To say the least, the U.S. team was a ragtag group.

The Americans not only had little time to practice— they played only one exhibition game prior to leaving for Brazil. It was a 1–0 loss to a touring team from England. In their previous seven international matches, American soccer teams had lost them all by a combined score of 45–2. No wonder Coach Bill Jeffrey told the media that "we have no chance."

In its first match of the World Cup, England beat Chile 2–0, and it was a harder match than expected. England featured an all-star team of great players nicknamed the "Kings of Football." England's star player was Stanley

American defenders Charlie Colombo and Walter Bahr go up for the ball against England's Thomas Finney.

ENGLAND VS UNITED STATES

COACH: Walter Winterbottom

CAPTAIN: Billy Wright

The English had a reputation as the "Kings of Football," with a post WWII record of 23 wins, 4 losses, and 3 draws

COACH: Bill Jeffrey

CAPTAIN: Walter Bahr

The USA team was made up entirely of amateurs who included a mailman, a paint-stripper, a dishwasher, and a hearse driver. The Americans had lost their last seven international matches by the combined score of 45–2

Matthews, who was widely considered to be one of the best soccer players in the world. But the English coach decided to save him for the really "tough games," so Matthews didn't play against Chile. And because the English thought they would easily beat the United States, Matthews didn't suit up against the Americans either.

The expectations among the U.S. players weren't much greater. Goaltender Frank Borghi said he hoped he could hold the English team to four or five goals.

Then the game began. As expected, England went on the attack. In the first 12 minutes of the game, the English had six good scoring chances. Two of those shots crashed off the goalpost. Surely it would be only a matter of time before England would score the first goal of the game. At the other end of the field, the Americans had taken exactly one shot on the English goalkeeper, Bert Williams.

Williams made an easy save. England continued to attack, and as the first half wore on, the English continued to take clear shots at the U.S. goal. But their shots either missed or were saved by goalie Frank Borghi.

In the 37th minute, for one of the rare times in the game, the U.S. team moved the ball onto England's side of the field. Walter Bahr took a shot from about 25 yards out on the right side. It was heading toward the far post, and the goalkeeper moved to his right to make an easy save. But before the ball got to him, Joe Gaetjens dove parallel to the ground and the ball deflected off his head. The ball then angled past goalkeeper Williams to his left and into the net. With just their second shot of the game, the Americans had taken a shocking 1–0 lead. There were eight minutes remaining in the first half, and the U.S. maintained its 1–0 lead for the remainder of the half.

The U.S. team was far from confident. At halftime, the players worried that the English would bombard them in the second half. There were still 45 minutes of soccer left. Early in the second half, the Americans had a good scoring chance, but Williams made the save for England. After that, the action was pretty much one sided. England was desperate to score the tying goal, but Frank Borghi was up to the task. And then came a crucial moment.

With just eight minutes to go, one of the English stars, Stan Mortensen, broke free and was heading toward the U.S. goal. Certainly, this would be the equalizer! But Charlie Colombo, a tough kid from St. Louis, caught Mortensen from behind and brought him down. England was awarded a free kick.

The kick was taken by another English star, Alf Ramsey. He chipped the ball over the U.S. line of defense, and the ball went right to his teammate Jimmy Mullen. Mullen headed it toward the goal, and it looked as if the ball were going into the net for sure, but at the last second, Frank Borghi deflected the ball away, preserving the 1–0 lead.

And then time ran out. The "no-hopers" had done it! They had dethroned the so-called "Kings of Football." England had dominated the action, but the United States

Joe Gaetjens is raised by cheering fans after the U.S. defeats England in the World Cup qualifier match.

scored the only goal of the game in a shocking 1–0 upset. The fans went wild. Many of them ran onto the field. They carried off the winning goal scorer, Joe Gaetjens, on their shoulders.

When the final score was sent out over the newswires, a British newspaper figured it had to be a misprint, so it published the final score as 10–1 in favor of England. That's how incredible it was. The Americans didn't win again that year; in fact, it would be 44 long years before the United States would win another World Cup soccer game. But as long as the sport is played, what a bunch of part-time American soccer players accomplished that day in Brazil will always be considered the biggest upset in soccer history.

LOS PEQUEÑOS GIGANTES

Kids take playing sports for granted. They just go outside and play ball. But not everywhere. This is the story of a scrappy bunch of kids who had never even watched their favorite sport on television nor had they seen their heroes play. But because of their own amazing accomplishments, they not only rose to the top of that sport, but they also got to meet those heroes in person.

After World War II, what is now known as the Little League World Series became a regular event in the small Pennsylvania town of Williamsport. In fact, a team from Williamsport won the very first championship in 1947. Thanks to that first tournament, the sport of Little League baseball really took off, expanding to every state and beyond. During the first 10 years of the Little League World Series, seven different states won the championship. Pennsylvania led the way with three; Connecticut was next with two. These days, Little League teams come from all over the world to compete, but during that first decade, it was mostly American

The 150-mile bus ride from Monterrey, Mexico, to McAllen, Texas.

teams and a couple of teams from Canada. In 1957 that changed in a major way.

In the industrial city of Monterrey, Mexico, a group of kids got interested in baseball. After church on Sunday, they would gather around the radio and listen to Brooklyn Dodgers baseball games being broadcast in Spanish from Ebbets Field in Brooklyn. They heard about such future Hall of Famers as Roy Campanella, Duke Snider, and Jackie Robinson. The kids could only imagine what they looked like as they tried to visualize the amazing things the Dodgers were doing on the baseball field.

The kids decided to emulate their heroes. They cleared rocks and glass off a field and created a baseball diamond. They played baseball barefoot with balls and gloves they made themselves. Cesar Faz worked in a steel mill in Monterrey. He had been born in San Antonio, Texas, and had been a batboy for a local team. He was one of the few people in town who knew anything about the game of baseball, so he gathered up the youngsters and coached them.

In July 1957, 14 kids and their coach came to America taking a 150-mile bus ride to McAllen, Texas. They were the Little League team representing Monterrey, Mexico. With three-day visas, they expected to play one baseball game and sightsee for the two other days. They packed light, with only the uniforms on their backs, a change of underwear, and very little money. The Monterrey kids played a team from Mexico City and beat them 9–2. And they kept on winning.

The U.S. ambassador to Mexico worked it out so the Monterrey players could stay in America as long as they won. Many of the kids were homesick, but they continued to play and win. They eventually won the Texas state championship, which earned them a trip to the Southern regional tournament in Louisville, Kentucky. That tournament would decide which team would go to Williamsport for the Little League World Series.

Monterrey not only didn't lose, they didn't allow a run. The kids from Monterrey beat Biloxi, Mississippi, 13–0 in the semifinal. In the final, they shut out Owensboro, Kentucky, 3–0. A bunch of poor kids from Mexico were the Southern regional champs. They had earned another bus ride—to Williamsport. And along the way, they picked up the nickname *Los Pequeños Gigantes*, which means "the Little Giants."

There were four teams competing in the 1957 Little League World Series. The other three were from Connecticut, Michigan, and California. Of the four teams, Monterrey was the youngest and the smallest. They were given brand-new baseball uniforms with the word *South* printed across their chests.

In the semifinal, Monterrey faced the East champion, Bridgeport, Connecticut. The game was scheduled for 2:30

Angel Macias pitched a perfect game to lead his team to the Little League World Championship.

in the afternoon. That was normally the time the Mexican kids would take a siesta, so they had to change their routine. Coach Faz got the boys up at 7:30 in the morning. They napped at 11 and then it was off to play Bridgeport to see who would go to the championship game.

Little League games are six innings long, and the game with Connecticut was scoreless until the fourth. It may have been Mexico's usual time to sleep, but it was Connecticut who got caught napping. Fidel Ruiz singled

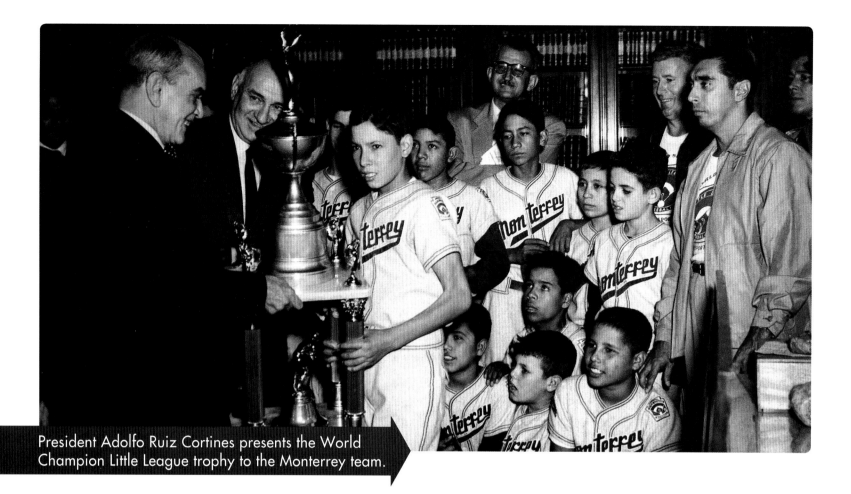

President Adolfo Ruiz Cortines presents the World Champion Little League trophy to the Monterrey team.

for Monterrey, and when he dashed to third base on another single, the Connecticut second baseman took the throw from the outfield and made a mistake. He didn't turn around to look at the infield, so Fidel took off from third and scored the game's first run. Monterrey scored two runs in the inning—enough to win the game 2–1. Pitcher Enrique Suarez threw a four-hitter.

In the other semifinal, California easily beat Michigan, 7–1. So the championship game was now all set. It was Monterrey, Mexico, against La Mesa, California.

On the mound for Monterrey was 12-year-old Angel Macias, all of 5 feet tall and weighing just 88 pounds. He had a full assortment of pitches: curves, sliders, and best of all, his fastball. Angel could do it all. He had played shortstop in the game against Bridgeport and had made some terrific plays. In fact, he could play all nine positions. He was the team's best fielder, batter, and pitcher.

Angel was not only a switch-hitter, but he was also ambidextrous, meaning he could throw with either arm. When he played first base, he did it as a lefty. Elsewhere in the infield, he played right-handed. And when he played in the outfield, he used whichever arm he felt like using. When Angel saw that California consisted of mostly righty batters, he decided to pitch right-handed so his curveball would break away from the hitters.

It was August 23, 1957. Ten thousand fans jammed the stadium in Williamsport. Back home in Monterrey, Mexico, people gathered in public squares to listen to the game on loudspeakers. What they heard, they couldn't believe. The Little Giants batted around in the fifth inning, scoring four runs. That was more than enough for their pint-sized pitcher, Angel Macias. He faced 18 California batters that afternoon in Williamsport. He struck out 11 of them. None of the other seven batters hit the ball out of the infield: 18 up, 18 down. A perfect game! It was the first perfect game ever pitched in a Little League championship game, and it hasn't been done since. When it was over, the players jumped around in celebration and Angel gave his coach a big hug. Back home in Mexico, fire engines raced through the streets with their sirens blaring. All of Monterrey was jubilant. Their kids had become the first foreign team to win the Little League World Series.

And their trip to the United States still wasn't over. It was off to Brooklyn to see their heroes play in person—the ones they had only heard about on the radio back home. They were guests of the Dodgers, who beat the St. Louis Cardinals, 6–5. The next day, they visited the White House and got to meet the president of the United States, Dwight Eisenhower. But the best was yet to come—a huge celebration back home in Mexico. They had gone from playing barefoot to becoming the champions of Little League baseball.

They were truly little giants.

The Monterrey Little League team shows their trophy to President Eisenhower.

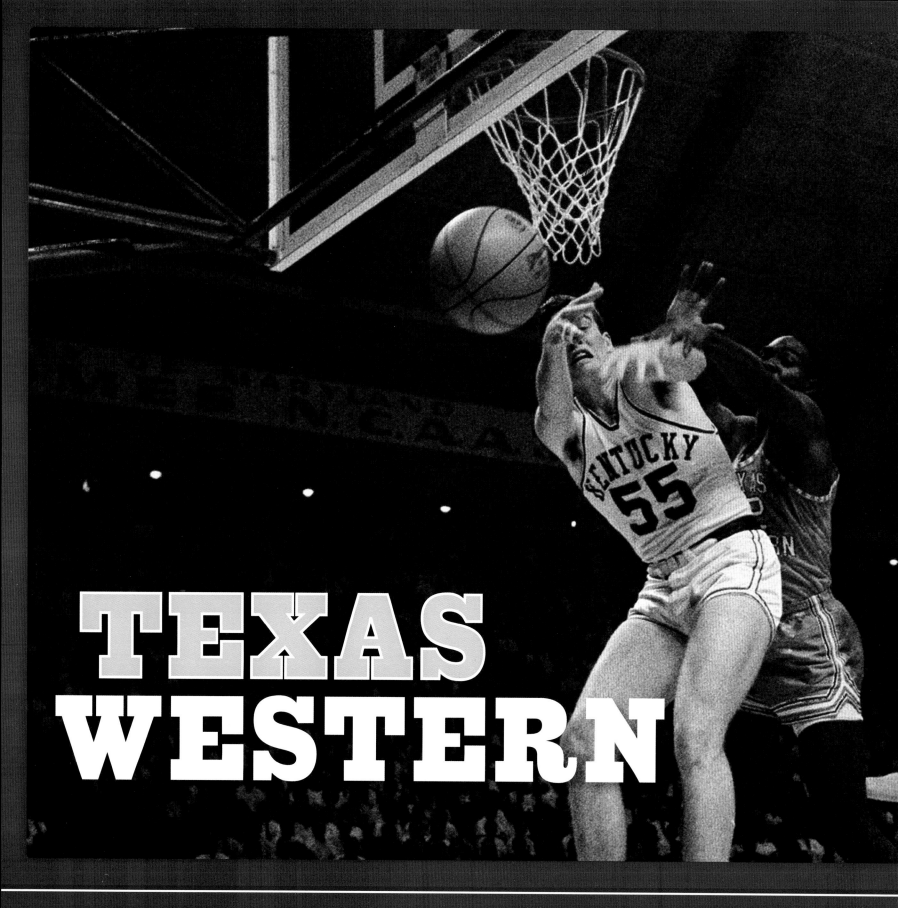

TEXAS WESTERN

n March 19, 1966, on the campus of the University of Maryland, something occurred that had never happened before. The entire starting basketball team playing in a national collegiate championship game was black. That team was Texas Western College, which is now known as the University of Texas at El Paso. At the time, segregation was a way of life in the South, and that extended to sports. Many teams wouldn't recruit black athletes, and if they did, some coaches would make sure there was always at least one white player in the starting lineup. Earlier that season, the Texas Western Miners had become the first team to break that "tradition." And now, in the championship game, their all-black starting lineup went up against the University of Kentucky Wildcats and their legendary coach, Adolph Rupp. Back then, he was the winningest coach in the history of college basketball. He had taken his team to the Final Four on four previous occasions, and each time, the Wildcats had won the tournament. Every single player on every one of his teams had been white, so for the 1966 NCAA Championship, five black starters faced off against an all-white team. It was historic.

The coach of Texas Western was Don Haskins, nicknamed "the Bear." When he came to Texas Western, it wasn't known for basketball. The school is located in El Paso in western Texas, near the Mexican border, and it was Haskins's job to convince basketball players to come there and play. It wasn't easy. Two years before Haskins arrived, the team's record had been 6–19. The Miners had never been invited to play in the NCAA tournament. But that changed in a hurry. In Haskins's first season, 1961–62, the Miners went 18 and 6. And in just his second year, Texas Western played in its first NCAA tournament.

Haskins recruited players that few other colleges wanted. Bobby Joe Hill was a 5'9" guard from near Detroit, Michigan. Kentucky coach Adolph Rupp said about Hill, "He's a good little boy, but there's a lot of good little boys around this year." Wait until you read what that "good little boy" did to Kentucky in that championship game.

David "Big Daddy" Lattin was the 6'6" center for the Miners. He grew up in Houston playing for a segregated all-black high school. Orsten Artis was a 6'1" guard from Gary, Indiana. Harry Flournay was also from Gary. He was a 6'5" forward. And for the championship game, Coach Haskins decided to start a third guard, Willie Worsley. He was just 5'6" and from the Bronx, New York. Those were the five black players who made history that night in Maryland.

Before the season began, nobody had picked Texas Western in the college basketball rankings. But the Miners played 10 games in December and won them all. Finally, people were starting to take notice. When the AP Top 10 basketball poll came out in January, Texas Western was listed for the first time in its history. The Miners were ranked ninth in the nation. By the time March came around, they were still undefeated. They went to Seattle, Washington, to play their final regular-season game. They were now 23–0 and ranked number two in the country. Seattle's record was a very average 15–10, but Seattle took the lead in the final minute and won the game 74–72. It was the Miners only loss all season.

Next up for Texas Western—the NCAA championships. The Miners entered the tournament ranked number three in the country. The number one ranked team was Kentucky. Texas Western opened things up with a fairly easy win against Oklahoma. Then the Miners survived in overtime against Cincinnati. Their next opponent was Kansas. The winner would go to the Final Four being played that year at the University of Maryland. What a game it was! In overtime, Kansas star Jo Jo White hit what looked like the game-winning shot,

Texas Western coach Don Haskins and team in a mid-game huddle but the referee ruled that White had stepped out of bounds, and the basket was waved off. So the game went to a second overtime. Led by Bobby Joe Hill's 22 points, the Miners won a double overtime thriller 81–80. Texas Western was now heading to the Final Four for the first time in school history.

The semifinals were all set. It would be Texas Western against Utah, while Kentucky would take on Duke. Most of the experts thought that whoever won the Kentucky–Duke game would win the national championship. Once again, the experts were wrong. In the Texas Western–Utah semifinal, Jerry Chambers scored 38 points for Utah. It was the most points any player had scored against Texas Western since Don Haskins became their coach. But one good player was not enough to beat the Miners team effort, and Texas Western won fairly easily, 85–78. Next up, the championship game against number one Kentucky.

This Texas Western team had never been to a championship game. So against a team that had come out of nowhere, it was expected that Adolph Rupp and his Wildcats would surely race past the Miners to win their fifth national championship. Well, Haskins had heard that Rupp vowed that a black team was never going to beat his Wildcats. Haskins told his players about it, and needless to say, they weren't happy. They couldn't wait to get at Kentucky.

Tommy Kron of Kentucky passes over Texas Western's David Lattin to teammate Larry Conley.

FAST FACT

None of the Wildcats were taller than 6'5". Because they lacked height, the team was known as "RUPP'S RUNTS."

So the game began. On their second possession, the Miners made a big impression. Center David Lattin took the ball and ferociously dunked it in with both hands, right over Wildcats forward Pat Riley. The Miners meant business. The game was close until midway through the first half—and then lightning struck. The Miners were leading 10–9 when the quick Bobby Joe Hill stole the ball away from Tommy Kron and went in for an easy layup. On the very next play, Hill did it again. He stole the ball from Louie Dampier and made another easy layup. Just like that, it was a five-point lead.

Early in the second half, Kentucky cut the Texas Western lead to one point, but the Miners stiffened on defense, and on offense, they went to the outside shot. Bobby Joe Hill and Orsten Artis quickly extended the lead. When David Lattin followed up a miss with a

Coach Don Haskins celebrates with his team after they win the NCAA championship.

basket, the Miners had themselves a 71–61 lead. They were now home free. Bobby Joe Hill led the way with 20 points, David Lattin had 16 points and nine rebounds, and Orsten Artis chipped in with 15. When the final buzzer sounded, the Miners had done it. They had won the NCAA championship, 72–65. They all hugged on the court as their fans

Texas Western's win was documented in the 2006 motion picture GLORY ROAD. Don Haskins appeared in the movie as an extra by playing a gas station attendant.

chanted "We're number one!" The players cut down the nets from the baskets—a championship tradition.

When they got home to El Paso, they were given a big parade in their honor. They had become the first college from Texas to win the NCAA tournament. In fact, they're still the only Texas school to have won it.

After that, the sport of college basketball was changed forever. Racial barriers came crashing down. Schools all over the South began recruiting black athletes. And that's why the historic NCAA Final in 1966 is considered by many to be the most important game in the history of college basketball.

LITTLE BIG MAN

I have no idea how many passes have been thrown in the history of college football, but I have a hunch which one is the most famous. It was thrown by Boston College quarterback Doug Flutie in 1984. It was a Hail Mary heave from a quarterback who wasn't very tall but whose stature grew larger and larger wherever he played football. Doug was a shade less than 5'10" tall, and he played his high school football in the Boston suburb of Natick, Massachusetts. He was constantly told he was too short to play major college football and that he should go to a smaller college to play. But he wouldn't listen, and in 1981, he was

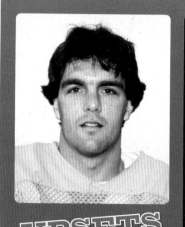

DOUG FLUTIE

BORN: October 23, 1962

BIRTHPLACE: Manchester, MD

HEIGHT: 5'10"

WEIGHT: 180 lbs.

TEAM: Boston College Eagles

POSITION: Quarterback

FAST FACT: Played briefly with his younger brother with the BC Lions in 1991

CAREER HIGHLIGHTS: Won the Heisman Trophy in 1984 and six-time winner of the CFL's Most Outstanding Player

offered a scholarship to play at nearby Boston College—the only major college that gave him a chance.

In his freshman year, Doug was listed as the fourth-string quarterback. But during the fourth game of the season, with the Boston College Eagles trailing Penn State 38–0, the coaches gave Doug Flutie a shot. He didn't disappoint. The first time he got the ball, he engineered a touchdown drive, completing all three passes he attempted. What a debut! And it only got better. In his sophomore year, he was the starting quarterback and he led Boston College to the Tangerine Bowl. It was the team's first bowl appearance in 40 years.

In his junior year, Doug broke the Boston College school passing record and was featured on the cover of *Sports Illustrated*. It was the first time in the history of Boston College that one of its athletes had been featured on the cover of the magazine. And there was another bowl game for the Eagles that year—the Liberty Bowl. Doug was also a finalist for the Heisman Trophy, which is awarded each year to the nation's most outstanding college football player. He didn't win it, but he was now considered the favorite to win the Heisman in his senior year. Flutie had a terrific college career, but the most famous moment of all was "the Pass."

At the Orange Bowl stadium in Miami, Florida, on November 23, 1984, the Eagles were facing the Miami Hurricanes. Boston College came into the game with a 7–2 record, ranked 10th in the nation. The Hurricanes were the defending national champions. They were 8–3 and ranked 12th. The two teams played the day after Thanksgiving, and the game was nationally televised. What a game it was! Both teams marched up and down the field and with just 28 seconds left, Miami scored to take a 45–41 lead.

Then there were just six seconds to go, and Boston College was 48 yards away from the end zone. On the radio, Dan Davis was the announcer. Here's how he called those final six seconds.

Here we go. Here's your ballgame, folks, as Flutie takes the snap. He drops straight back, has some time, now he scrambles away from one hit, looks, uncorks a deep one for the end zone. Phelan is there.

He did it! Touchdown! Touchdown! Touchdown! Touchdown! Touchdown, Boston College! He did it! He did it! Flutie did it! He hit Phelan in the end zone. Touchdown. Oh my goodness!

It was a 48-yard, last-ditch Hail Mary pass that was caught in the end zone by Doug's roommate, wide receiver Gerard Phelan. It was Phelan's 11th catch of the afternoon, and it won the game for Boston College, 47–45. That day, Doug Flutie became the first college quarterback to pass for more than 10,000 yards in a career—just one more amazing accomplishment for a kid who was supposedly "too small" to play at a major college.

One week later, Doug won the Heisman Trophy. He was now the best player in all of college football. And then, on New Year's Day, he threw three touchdown passes as the Eagles beat Houston in the Cotton Bowl, 45-28. It was Boston College's first bowl win in 44 years! What a way to cap off a college career!

But Doug wasn't finished playing football. Again, the critics said he was too small to play in the NFL. He may have received the award as the best player in college football, but NFL teams thought that 284 other players were better and drafted them before Doug. The Los Angeles Rams finally selected him in the 11th round. At the time, a rival football league had come into existence, called

Doug Flutie and his teammates celebrate after winning the Orange Bowl in 1984.

the United States Football League (USFL), and instead of signing with the Rams in the NFL, Doug decided to play in the USFL for the New Jersey Generals. But the USFL folded the following year, and Doug joined the NFL, bouncing from the Chicago Bears to the New England Patriots.

LISTEN to this MOMENT TRACK 8

By the end of the 1989 season, Doug had been out of college for five years. In his four NFL seasons, he appeared in a total of 22 games and threw 14 touchdown passes. He had also been intercepted 16 times. The Patriots released him. When no other NFL team showed an interest, it looked like the end of the line for Doug, but then his career took another big turn—north.

Doug went to play in the Canadian Football League (CFL). Not a bad move. He proceeded to rewrite the CFL record book. In his second season with the B.C. Lions, he threw for a record 6,619 yards. The following year, he signed with another CFL team, the Calgary Stampeders. He led Calgary to a victory in the 1992 Grey Cup, the CFL championship game. He set another record in 1994, throwing for 48 touchdowns. And when he signed with his third CFL team, the Toronto Argonauts, he led them to back-to-back championships in 1996 and 1997.

All in all, Doug played eight seasons in Canada and was named the CFL's Most Outstanding Player six times! He won three championships and was named the Grey Cup MVP all three times. When a poll was taken to determine the greatest player in the history of the CFL, Doug Flutie won that too. And to top it off, he was voted into Canada's

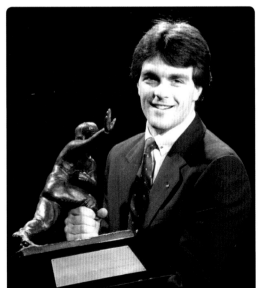

Doug Flutie poses with the Heisman trophy in 1984, the trophy for CFL's Most Outstanding Player in 1997, and his induction plaque into the College Football Hall of Fame in 2007.

Sports Hall of Fame—the first non-Canadian so honored. At age 35, he had done everything he could possibly do on a football field in Canada. But guess what? It wasn't over!

In 1998 Doug once again signed to play in the NFL, this time with the Buffalo Bills. The NFL was the only place Flutie had never enjoyed great success. That was about to change. He took over for injured Bills quarterback Rob Johnson in the fifth game of the season and led Buffalo to a win in Indianapolis. The following week, he started an NFL game for the first time in nine years. With 13 seconds left, he ran into the end zone to score the winning touchdown, handing Jacksonville its first loss of the season. Flutie and Buffalo kept on winning, and he led the Bills into the playoffs. They wound up losing to Miami, but Doug was voted the NFL Comeback Player of the Year, and he was picked to play in the Pro Bowl, the NFL's all-star game. Once again, he had proved all the doubters wrong.

The following year, Doug led the Bills to an 11–5 record and another playoff appearance. But in a controversial decision, Rob Johnson was chosen to start instead of Doug in Buffalo's playoff game against Tennessee. The Bills lost that game, and many believe that if Flutie had started, the result would have been different.

After that, Doug suited up five more years with Buffalo and San Diego and then returned to the New England Patriots for one last season. The final play of his 21-year career occurred on January 1, 2006. At age 43, he was

Doug Flutie stands beside an image of himself on a box of Wheaties.

the oldest player in the NFL. That day, he drop-kicked an extra point. You read that correctly. A kicker doesn't have to kick an extra point with another player holding the ball. The kicker can take the snap directly, drop the ball to the ground, let it bounce once, and then kick it through the uprights for an extra point. That's what Doug did. It was the first time a dropkick had been converted in the NFL in 65 years! So the quarterback who delivered "the Pass" had now added a rare dropkick to his résumé. Was there anything Doug Flutie couldn't do?

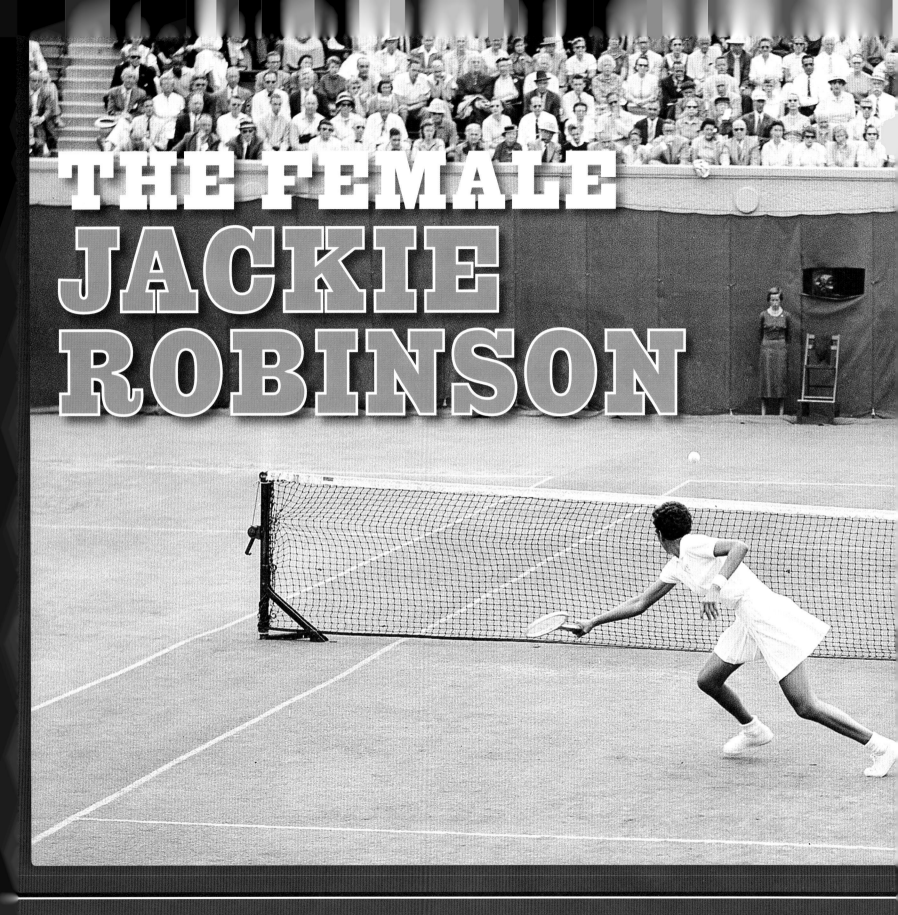

THE FEMALE JACKIE ROBINSON

When you've seen Venus or Serena Williams win one of their many tennis championships, you probably never gave it a second thought. But there was a time when a black woman playing tennis was anything but commonplace. In every sport, there are black athletes who were the first to break the so-called "color barrier," the most famous being Jackie Robinson in baseball. So it's no wonder that Althea Gibson is called "the Jackie Robinson of tennis." Not only was she the first black woman to play at Wimbledon and the U.S. Open, but she was also the first black player period. On top of that, tennis was thought of as a "country club sport"—a sport that was only enjoyed by "rich people." Althea Gibson was anything but.

Althea grew up in a poor neighborhood in Harlem, New York City. At the time, America was struggling through the Great Depression. Her parents were on welfare, and she would often play hooky from school, getting into fights with other kids. On a couple of occasions, she ran away from home. It's hard to imagine that such a difficult upbringing spawned a trailblazing championship tennis career. But one summer, when she was 10 years old, the street was closed off right in front of her apartment so the kids could play. A paddle tennis court was built directly across from her building. It was smaller than a real tennis court, and instead of playing with racquets, players used solid paddles. Althea loved it. It seemed as if they had built the court just for her. It wasn't long before she was noticed and given the opportunity to play at a local tennis club. She of course couldn't afford to join, but club members were so impressed with her ability that they purchased a membership for her. She took lots of lessons and decided to play in tournaments. Back then, what is now known as the United States Tennis Association (USTA) did not allow black players to enter its tournaments, so

ALTHEA GIBSON

BORN: August 25, 1927

BIRTHPLACE: Silver, SC

HEIGHT: 5'11"

PLAYS: right-handed

TURNED PRO: 1950

NICKNAME: "the Jackie Robinson of tennis"

UPSETS AND UNDERDOGS

CAREER HIGHLIGHTS: Won the French Open in 1956; U.S. Open in 1957 and 1958; Wimbledon in 1957 and 1958; was inducted into the International Tennis Hall of Fame in 1971

Althea began playing in American Tennis Association (ATA) tournaments, which catered to black players. At age 15, she played in her very first state tournament, and she won it!

By now, Althea was a high school dropout living on welfare, but her tennis had caught the attention of two surgeons from Wilmington, North Carolina. They liked to help promising young black tennis players. So she moved to North Carolina to live with the doctors. They paid all her expenses while she worked on her game. Perhaps more importantly, she went back to high school. Along with her tennis, she now took her schoolwork seriously, graduating 10th in her class. She received a scholarship to go to Florida A&M University. But she also learned about something else in the South—segregation. Blacks in the South were forced to sit in the back of the bus, and Althea didn't like it one bit.

Althea's tennis continued to improve, and she started competing in ATA national tournaments. She was unbeatable. From 1947 through 1956, she won the ATA championship every year—10 straight. But she was still having trouble getting into the major white tournaments. In order to play in the U.S. National Championships at Forest Hills, which is now known as the U.S. Open, she had to play in United States Lawn Tennis Association (USLTA) events, but because of her race, she wasn't allowed to play. However, segregation was ending in the other sports. Jackie Robinson was now a star for the Brooklyn Dodgers, and black players were making a big impact in basketball and football. It was only a matter of time before tennis would also integrate.

Finally, in 1950, after many people, including former tennis champions, put pressure on the tennis establishment, Althea Gibson was given her chance. She took the subway to Forest Hills and walked onto the grass courts to play her first match at the U.S. National Championships. Here's what the *New York Times* wrote the next day:

Althea Gibson returns a serve at Wimbledon.

That was it. Althea had made history, but the event was given just one paragraph buried at the end of the newspaper column. She also played a strong second-round match against Louise Brough, who was the reigning three-time Wimbledon champion. Brough won it 9–7 in the third set. Althea's tournament was over, but tennis fans had taken notice. The following summer, she also made history at Wimbledon, becoming the first black tennis player to compete in that famed tournament. Again, she didn't disappoint. She made it to the third round before losing to the fifth-seeded player.

Tennis's major barriers had been broken through, but the fans and the media were looking for much more from Althea. They wanted to see her win. The critics were starting to say she "couldn't win the big one." But that all changed in 1956. Althea was 28 years old when she entered the French Open in Paris, France. She not only won the singles, but she won in doubles too. She had now

ALTHEA GIBSON didn't stop at breaking the color barrier in tennis. She also became the **FIRST AFRICAN AMERICAN WOMAN** to play golf on the **LPGA** tour!

become the first black tennis player to win a major tennis tournament. From there, it was on to England, where she won the Wimbledon doubles title. That was yet another first for Althea—she was the first black player of either sex to win a Wimbledon championship of any kind. That year, she also made it to the U.S. National Championships finals before losing in straight sets. It was quite a year for her—but 1957 was even better.

On a 96-degree July day in 1957, she took to Centre Court at Wimbledon to take on fellow American Darlene Hard in the finals. It was no contest. With big serves and great volleys at the net, Althea clinched the championship in two straight sets. It took just 50 minutes. Queen Elizabeth II presented her with the winning trophy, and when she returned home, she was given a big ticker tape parade in New York City. She sat on the back of a convertible, riding up Broadway while being cheered by thousands. She was then honored at a luncheon at the famed Waldorf Astoria Hotel—a far cry from her poor childhood uptown in Harlem.

Next up was the U.S. National Championships, and this time, she won. It was another easy straight-sets victory, beating Louise Brough in the final. She was the woman who beat Althea in her U.S. National Championships debut. Althea Gibson was now the reigning queen of tennis. For good measure, she also won the Wimbledon and U.S. titles the following year. All in all, the young girl who wasn't allowed to play in "white" tournaments went on to win five major singles tennis championships.

Maybe what Althea said about winning her first Wimbledon singles title summed it up best: "Shaking hands with the Queen of England was a long way from being forced to sit in the colored section of the bus going into downtown Wilmington, N.C." That it was, and it was quite a journey. She had paved the way for generations of young black tennis players who were to follow. Althea Gibson didn't just break down barriers—she smashed them to pieces.

Althea Gibson holds her National Tennis Championship trophy alongside men's winner, Mal Anderson.

RIDE 'EM, COWBOYS

I f you go online and search for "craziest football game ever," highlights will pop up from the 2007 Fiesta Bowl. I'll let you decide if it's indeed the zaniest of all time, but I dare you to find another college football game that featured a wilder comeback with more trick plays. And to top it all off, the game ended with a marriage proposal! But I'm getting way ahead of myself.

It was New Year's Day in Glendale, Arizona. The two teams playing that day couldn't have been more different. The Oklahoma Sooners are one of the oldest and most

Boise State charges onto the field at the start of the Fiesta Bowl.

record, but even so, they were only ranked ninth in the country by the Associated Press. In 2006 the Cowboys played in the Western Athletic Conference, and their conference and their schedule weren't considered as difficult as the teams ranked ahead of them. Oklahoma, despite its two losses, was ranked higher, at seventh. The oddsmakers weren't impressed with the Cowboys perfect record either. They predicted the Sooners would win the Fiesta Bowl by seven to eight points.

successful teams in college football history. They've been playing college football at the University of Oklahoma for more than 100 years. They are known for seven national championships and a record 47 straight wins between 1953 and 1957. Their opponents, the Boise State Cowboys, had been playing major college football for only a decade, and they are best known for their home stadium in Boise, Idaho. They have a blue artificial field, nicknamed "Smurf Turf." When it comes to traditional rivalries, this wasn't even close.

Oklahoma arrived at the Fiesta Bowl with an 11–2 record. The 2006 Boise State Cowboys had a perfect 12–0

More than 78,000 fans jammed into the stands that New Year's Day night. The Cowboys were led onto the field by a horse as their band played. The Sooners were led onto the field by a covered wagon driven by two horses. There was definitely a Western flavor, but on FOX television, the announcers viewed it as biblical. They called it "David versus Goliath" and pointed out that everybody outside of the state of Oklahoma was rooting for underdog Boise State.

Midway through the first quarter, Ian Johnson ran two yards for a touchdown, and the Cowboys led the favored

Sooners 14–0. In the third quarter, when defensive back Marty Tadman intercepted a pass and ran it 17 yards for a touchdown, Boise State had a commanding 28–10 lead. Then things turned around, and Oklahoma went on a tear. With just 1:26 left in the game, the Sooners tied it at 28.

On the first play after the ensuing kickoff, Boise State quarterback Jared Zabransky threw a pass right into the hands of Oklahoma defensive back Marcus Walker, who ran untouched 33 yards for a touchdown. Oklahoma had scored 25 unanswered points, taking its first lead of the game, 35–28. Boise State fans were stunned and in disbelief. With just 62 seconds remaining, it looked like the Sooners had dashed their hopes of a major upset.

After the next kickoff, the Cowboys moved the ball to midfield, and it all came down to one final play. There were 18 seconds remaining in the game, and Boise State was facing a fourth down with 18 yards to go, 50 yards away from the end zone. What happened next has various names in football. Some call it the "hook and ladder play." More accurately, it's a "hook

LISTEN to this MOMENT TRACK 9

and lateral." In Boise State's playbook, it went by the simple name *circus*. Perfect.

Quarterback Jared Zabransky, who had just thrown that critical interception, dropped back to pass, and he threw it 15 yards over the middle to wide receiver Drisan James. James then took a couple of strides to his right, drawing the defense in that direction, and at that very moment, he lateraled the ball behind him to Jerard Rabb, who took off to the left. Oklahoma chased him down as he neared the goal line, and at the last moment, Rabb dove into the end zone.

Boise State quarterback hands off the ball to tailback Ian Johnson.

The extra-point kick was good. Boise State had tied the game 35–35 in miraculous fashion. The Fiesta Bowl was now heading to overtime.

In college football's overtime, each team gets one possession from the other team's 25-yard line. The team that's ahead after each has had a turn wins the game. If it's still tied, they both go again. Boise State won the coin toss and decided to play defense first, so Oklahoma began with the ball on the Cowboys 25-yard line. The ball was handed to Adrian Peterson, and he ran the entire 25 yards for a touchdown. The extra-point attempt was good. Just like that, Oklahoma led 42–35.

Now it was the Cowboys turn. They needed a touchdown and an extra point to force a second overtime. Again, they faced a critical do-or-die situation. They drove the ball down to the 5-yard line, but now it was fourth down and two yards to go for a first down. Did they have another trick up their sleeves? Absolutely.

Before the snap, the quarterback ran to his left, and the center snapped the ball directly to wide receiver Vinny Perretta.

Ian Johnson runs in the two-point conversion, winning the Fiesta Bowl for Boise State.

After the win, Ian Johnson proposes to his girlfriend, cheerleader Chrissy Popadics.

Vinny ran to his right, slowed down, and then lofted a short pass to tight end Derek Schouman. Touchdown! It was the first time Perretta had thrown a pass all season. The Cowboys were one point away from tying the game—but then their first-year coach, Chris Petersen, made a crucial decision. He would go for two points. They couldn't possibly have a third trick play, could they?

The play they used is called the "Statue of Liberty" play. The quarterback pretends to throw a pass with one arm in the air, but the ball is in his other hand, down at his side. So while he looks like he's throwing with one arm, he's actually handing the ball off to a running back with his other hand.

That's what the Cowboys attempted. What a spot to try it! If it worked, they would score two points and win the game. If it flopped, they would lose. Quarterback Jared Zabransky went back to pass. He faked a throw to the right with his empty right hand. Then he handed the ball off with his left hand to running back Ian Johnson. Ian ran to the left, untouched, into the end zone. Thanks to three trick plays, Boise State won the Fiesta Bowl 43–42! It was the biggest win in school history, capping a perfect 13–0 season. But for Ian Johnson, it wasn't perfect yet.

After his dramatic run had won the game for Boise State, Ian was being interviewed on national television. He got down on one knee and proposed to his cheerleader girlfriend, Chrissy Popadics. She said yes. Now it was perfect.

THE GREAT AMERICAN RACE

Can you imagine driving a car around in circles for four hours? That's what 20-year-old Trevor Bayne did—and for his efforts, he won $1.463 million. Not too shabby. Of course, he wasn't just riding around by himself. There were 42 other drivers racing on the same track. And it wasn't just any ordinary race. It was the biggest and most prestigious race in all of NASCAR: the 2011 Daytona 500. The first Daytona 500 was staged in Daytona Beach, Florida, in 1959. Over the years, it gained the nickname "the Great American Race," and some legendary drivers have won. "The King," Richard Petty, won the race an astounding seven times. More recently, Jeff Gordon took the checkered flag on three occasions. But what happened in the 2011 race stunned everybody.

Trevor Bayne was born February 19, 1991, in Knoxville, Tennessee. His father bought him a go-kart when he was five years old. He knew exactly what he wanted to be when he grew up—he dreamed of becoming a race-car driver. So he set off racing. He competed for eight years on the go-kart circuit—and talk about success! He won more than 300 races and three world championships. It was time to step up in class.

Next was the Allison Legacy Race Series. That's for teenagers, and they race cars that are three-quarters the size of NASCAR cars. Trevor kept on winning. At age 13, he was named the Rookie of the Year—the youngest to ever win that award. During his two years in the series, he won 14 races, including the national championship when he was 14. He was well on his way. Next up: full-sized cars on short tracks. Again, Trevor won Rookie of the Year honors. Throughout his young life, the pattern was the same. Wherever he showed up to drive, he quickly made a name for himself—all the way to the Daytona 500.

At age 17, Trevor won his first NASCAR series race, which is kind of like the minor leagues of NASCAR. Over the next three years, he continued to race and continued to improve, but he didn't win any more races. That's why what happened at Daytona was so unexpected. It was only his second Sprint Cup start. The Sprint Cup is the major leagues of NASCAR,

TREVOR BAYNE

BORN: February 19, 1991

BIRTHPLACE: Knoxville, TN

CAR NUMBER: 21

RACING TEAM: Wood Brothers

CAREER HIGHLIGHTS: Won the Daytona 500 in 2011

in which the best drivers compete in the biggest races for the most prize money. In November 2010, at age 19, Trevor made his "major league" debut. He raced in the Texas 500 and completed every lap. It was a big accomplishment for a young driver. Of the 43 drivers that day, Trevor finished 17th. Not bad—but still, very few people had heard of him. That was about to change big-time.

On February 18, 2011, Trevor celebrated his 20th birthday. The next day, he raced in the 53rd Daytona 500. Most people believed that big names like Dale Earnhardt Jr.,

A multi-car crash takes Michael Waltrip, Andy Lally, Joe Nemechek, Greg Biffle, David Reutimann, Jimmie Johnson, Mark Martin, and Jeff Gordon out of the race.

Jeff Gordon, and Jimmie Johnson had a good chance to win. But Trevor Bayne—in just his second Sprint Cup race and his very first Daytona 500? No chance.

More than 175,000 fans jammed into the Daytona International Speedway. To call what followed *wild* would be a major understatement. It was more like "the Crazy American Race." The cars line up in twos, and because Trevor had qualified 32nd out of 43, he was well back at the start.

There was a new style of racing that year. The drivers decided that the fastest way around the track was to pair up. The car behind would literally push the car in front. They would switch positions every few laps because of the wear and tear on the engine that was doing the pushing. This all led to a major accident on the 29th lap. Cars were crashing all over the place—14 in all. Some of the biggest names were knocked out of the race, including three-time winner Jeff Gordon and Jimmie Johnson. And so it went.

There was something else that was fairly new in car racing. In the past, when there were accidents, races would be allowed to finish under the yellow caution flag. While a yellow flag is up, drivers aren't allowed to pass other cars. But they changed the rules. They would

Sprint Driver Trevor Bayne holds the lead heading into the final lap of the 2011 Daytona 500.

LISTEN to this MOMENT TRACK 10

no longer end a race under a yellow flag. If drivers had reached 500 miles and there was a yellow flag, they would keep going until a green flag came out for normal racing. Once the green flag came out, they would then have to race two more laps. And that's exactly what happened—twice. As a result, the Daytona 500 in 2011 was really the Daytona 520. They had to race 20 extra miles!

Other records broken during the race that Trevor won: There were 16 DIFFERENT YELLOW CAUTION FLAGS because of accidents. There were 74 LEAD CHANGES, with 22 DIFFERENT DRIVERS LEADING at one time or another.

Trevor Bayne coasts over the finish line to win the Daytona 500.

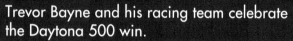

Trevor Bayne and his racing team celebrate the Daytona 500 win.

The first time the drivers were set to start the two-lap sprint to the finish, David Ragan started too soon and was disqualified. Meanwhile, there was another accident back in the pack, so they had to start again. This time, with just two laps to go, it was rookie Trevor Bayne in the lead. And with one lap to go, he was still in the lead. In fact, there were three groupings of two cars. Bayne was being pushed by Bobby Labonte. Right behind them, Kurt Busch was being pushed by Juan Pablo Montoya. And just behind them were Carl Edwards and his pusher, David Gilliland. As they neared the final turn, Edwards and Gilliland made their move. They blew past the second grouping and were right behind Bayne and Labonte. Coming out of the fourth turn, it was a mad dash to the finish line. Trevor broke free of his pusher. Carl Edwards was right on his tail. Could Trevor hold him off? The answer was a resounding *yes*. Trevor took the checkered flag, becoming the youngest winner in the history of the Daytona 500. The TV announcer screamed something about Cinderella. Trevor was screaming too, into his radio, yelling "Are you kidding me?"

It was time for Trevor to drive to Victory Lane, the winner's circle. Trevor had never driven there before at Daytona, so he actually had to ask for directions. When he finally got there, he said, "I keep thinking I'm dreaming." He wasn't. His dream had ended—it had come true.

MICHAEL CHANG

Have you ever heard of Roland Garros Stadium? It's in Paris, and it's home to the French Open tennis tournament in late May. It's the only Grand Slam tennis tournament played on clay. The U.S. and Australian Opens are played on hard surfaces, while Wimbledon is on grass. American men haven't fared very well on the red clay of Roland Garros. There have been some great U.S. tennis champs over the years, such as Pete Sampras, John McEnroe, and Jimmy Connors. Among them, they've won 29 Grand Slam singles titles—but not one French Open. Tony Trabert won the French Open in 1955, and it took 34 long years for another American to win it. The player who finally broke that long drought was a huge surprise. Not only was he just 17 years old, but he was also not particularly big—under 6 feet tall. He was often compared with the biblical David taking on much bigger Goliaths.

Michael Chang was born in Hoboken, New Jersey, in 1972. The Chang family moved to Minnesota, where Michael started playing tennis at age six. His older brother Carl was a tennis player too, and the family next moved to California, where the boys could play year-round in outdoor tournaments. Michael's career really took off. When he was 12, he won his first national title: the USTA Junior Hardcourt Championships.

In 1987 Michael won two major tournaments for boys under 18. First he won the USTA Hardcourt Championships and then he took the Nationals by storm in Kalamazoo, Michigan. He was seeded sixth, and in the finals, he beat the number two seed, Jim Courier. Michael was just 15 years old, and he became the youngest player to ever win the event. More importantly, by winning in Kalamazoo, he qualified for the U.S. Open.

In his first-round match, he played Paul McNamee. It was a 15-year-old amateur taking on a 32-year-old pro, and Michael won in four sets. He was now the youngest player to ever win a match at the U.S. Open. American tennis fans were thirsting for a new champion to emerge. The members of the old guard, John McEnroe and Jimmy Connors, were nearing the ends of their careers. One newspaper had the headline, "Is a new U.S. star rising?" When McEnroe followed Michael into the interview room after Michael's historic win, McEnroe said, "Michael Chang? Who's Michael Chang?" McEnroe and everyone else would soon find out. And while Michael lost his second-round match, he wasn't finished setting records.

The next year, at age 16, he turned pro, and at the 1986 French Open, guess who he got to play in the third round? John McEnroe. But McEnroe easily beat him. Could it be that Michael's success had finally come to an end? Nobody could have predicted what would happen the following year at Roland Garros.

Michael was now 17 as he played in the 1989 French

The Roland Garros Stadium center court filled to capacity during the final between Michael Chang and Stefan Edberg.

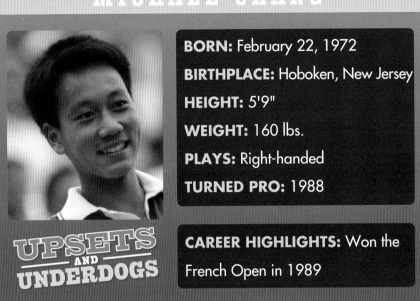

MICHAEL CHANG

BORN: February 22, 1972

BIRTHPLACE: Hoboken, New Jersey

HEIGHT: 5'9"

WEIGHT: 160 lbs.

PLAYS: Right-handed

TURNED PRO: 1988

CAREER HIGHLIGHTS: Won the French Open in 1989

Open. In the fourth round, he met up with the number one player in the world, Ivan Lendl. Lendl won the year's first Grand Slam tournament, the Australian Open, and he had already won three French Opens. Chang didn't present much of a threat. But what happened over the next four hours and 38 minutes is now part of tennis lore.

It looked like it would be a rout. Lendl won the first set in the best of five, 6–4. He also won the second set by the same score. Lendl was dominating. One more set, and Michael would be finished. But it never happened. With the score tied at three games apiece in the third set, Michael turned things around. He and Lendl engaged in long rallies, and Michael kept winning points. Michael won the next three games to capture the third set, 6–3.

It was the first set that Lendl had lost in the tournament. And then Michael won the fourth set, also 6–3. That set up a decisive fifth set. It was epic.

Michael's legs were cramping. He had grown weak and was having trouble running. He had to constantly drink water. At times, he couldn't even sit down between games. Michael thought about quitting, but he hung in there. He kept hitting high lobs called "moon balls." He did whatever he could to get the ball back over the net. At the opportune moment, Michael would blast a hard shot. The strategy was working. Lendl was making mistakes.

Again, the set was three games apiece, and Michael eked out the next game to take a 4–3 lead. Just two more games, and he'd survive to the quarterfinals.

In the next game, Michael did something that shocked the tennis world. When he would reach up to hit his serve, his legs would cramp up. So at one point, he served the ball underhand. Nobody had seen that before at such a critical point in a match—a soft underhand serve. Lendl's return wasn't very strong, and Michael hit a hard shot to Lendl's backhand that he couldn't return. Point for Michael Chang. That was the major turning point. Michael won the next point to take a 5–3 lead. Just one more game to go.

Lendl was now serving, but Michael was in control. With the score 15–40, Lendl's first serve was long. His second serve then clipped the net and also landed long.

Michael collapsed to the clay. He had somehow won a five-set marathon. The TV announcer was saying "I don't believe it!" The crowd was standing and roaring. Fans had witnessed one of the most amazing matches in tennis history. Michael, who at times could barely move, had knocked off the number one player in the world and advanced to the quarterfinals. He walked off the court in tears of joy and exhaustion.

In the quarterfinals, Michael faced Ronald Agenor from Haiti. Michael won a fourth-set tiebreaker 8–6 to win the match 3 sets to 1. Next, the semifinals—another marathon.

Michael Chang celebrates after winning a major point in the final match of the French Open.

It took four hours and five minutes. Michael beat Andrei Chesnokov of the Soviet Union in four sets to advance to the finals of the French Open. Another huge test awaited Michael. He was up against the number three seed, Sweden's Stefan Edberg. Edberg had already won three Grand Slam titles and would win three more in his Hall of Fame career.

In the final, Edberg took a 2–1 lead in sets. Michael once again had to come from behind. Edberg rushed the net, but Michael's returns were terrific. He smashed some great passing shots. Michael won the fourth set, once again setting up a decisive fifth set. Despite all that Michael had been through, he appeared to be the fresher player. There was no cramping this time, and Michael easily hit a shot he had developed: a jumping, two-handed backhand. Finally, Edberg hit a shot into the net, and it was over. Michael had taken the fifth set 6–2 to win the French Open—the first American man to do so since 1955.

Afterward, Michael couldn't explain how he had done it. He said that maybe it was a little luck. But it was much more than that. It was his courageous, never-say-die attitude that lifted him to a place that nobody predicted. At age 17, he was a major champion. A new era had dawned in American tennis. Soon, Pete Sampras, Andre Agassi, and Jim Courier would all make their mark. An American tennis resurgence had been started by Michael Chang, who to this day remains the youngest man to ever win a Grand Slam tennis tournament.

JASON MCELWAIN

he year 2006 featured some terrific basketball. Kobe Bryant of the Los Angeles Lakers scored 81 points in a game against Toronto. It was the most an NBA player had scored in a game since Wilt Chamberlain scored 100 all the way back in 1962. In college basketball that year, a true Cinderella team, George Mason University, made it to the Final Four but lost in the semifinal to the eventual champion, Florida. However, the most amazing basketball story of all involved a player who wasn't in the NBA—nor was he even a college basketball star. In fact, he was barely on his high school team. His name is Jason McElwain, and his entire varsity playing career lasted all of 259 seconds. But what an incredible four minutes and 19 seconds it was!

Jason McElwain shoots another three-pointer.

Jason grew up in Rochester, New York. When he was two years old, he was diagnosed with autism. He didn't speak until he was five. For Jason, it was no big deal. He said, "I'm just normal like other people—that's the way I am." He is high-functioning autistic, meaning he can do lots of things, but in school, he had to take special education courses. When he got to Greece Athena High School, he wanted to play basketball. He didn't make the junior varsity team, but to stay involved in basketball, he became the team's student manager. And J-Mac, as he was called, was a great manager. His job, as he put it, was to hand out water and towels to the players and to act enthusiastic. He had no problem with any of that. He supported his team and was there for every game to help cheer them on. He was the manager for three seasons. And now his high school days were nearing an end.

The date was February 15, 2006. It was Senior Night, the last home game of Jason's senior year in high school. Greece Athena was taking on nearby Spencerport High School. Coach Jim Johnson told Jason that he was going to let him suit up for the game. He might not get to play, but at least for one game, he could proudly wear the uniform of the Greece Athena Trojans. Many of the kids at school heard that Jason would be on the bench, so they showed up at the game with pictures of Jason that they held on sticks in front of their faces like masks, so they could all be Jason. He had his own personal cheering section in the stands. As the game wore on, they started chanting "J-Mac! J-Mac!"

With 4:19 left in the game, the Trojans were leading by 28 points. Coach Johnson stood up, pointed at No. 52, and told him he was going into the game. No. 52 was Jason McElwain. For the first time, he was going to play for the Greece Athena Trojans. Jason's cheering section saw what was happening, and they all stood up, roaring their approval. Actually, as Jason described it, they were: "Wild, nuts, crazy, whatever you want to call it." If there is one trait about Jason, he isn't shy—on or off the court.

Moments after Jason got into the game, he was passed the ball deep in the right corner. He immediately threw up a long three-point shot and missed badly. It was an air ball. Back on the bench, Coach Johnson put his head in his hands. He said to himself, "Dear God, please just get him one basket." A few seconds later, J-Mac took another shot, and he missed that one too. But Jason isn't one to give up. His teammates kept passing him the ball. They wanted him to shoot—so shoot he did.

The next time Jason got the ball, he fired up another long three-point shot from the right side and—*swish!* Three

High school basketball star Jason McElwain celebrates after being recognized at a New York Knicks game in 2006.

points! The moment the ball went in, his teammates on the bench jumped up in the air to celebrate. Coach Johnson thought, "Oh my God, my dream for him has come true." The coach was fighting back tears. In the stands, it was sheer bedlam, especially in J-Mac's cheering section. What happened next? Jason said, "I caught fire. I was hot as a pistol." No, he wasn't just hot—he was sizzling.

He took another three-point shot and—*swish!* Then another. Good again. He took shot after shot, most of them three-pointers, and one after another, they went in. As the final seconds ticked away, the Trojans came down for one final shot. Who would take it? Jason, of course. And again—*swish!* Greece Athena won the game 79–43. Jason made six three-pointers and totaled 20 points. He was only in the game for a little more than four minutes, and but he was his team's high scorer. Not only that, but his six three-pointers had tied the school record!

As soon as the game ended, the fans and players rushed onto the court. They mobbed the game's unlikely hero, Jason McElwain. They picked up J-Mac and put him on their shoulders. After that, he posed for pictures with the cheerleaders and even signed autographs. What a scene! It was something right out of a Hollywood movie. In school, Jason was an instant celebrity. Teachers stopped to shake his hand. Jason said even the pretty girls who wouldn't talk to him before were now saying hello.

The story of what happened that night was shown on television all over the country. One of the people watching happened to live in the White House: President George W. Bush. When he saw the news about Jason, he cried, pretty much like everyone else who saw it.

A few weeks later, the president was heading to upstate New York, and he just had to meet Jason. He had Air Force One land at the Rochester airport. As he walked off the plane, he was greeted by Jason and his parents. The president said that Jason's story was "the story of a young man who found his touch on the basketball court, which in turn touched the hearts of citizens all across the country." It certainly did.

Jason McElwain is presented with a trophy by actor Jake Gyllenhaal for best moment at the 2006 ESPY Awards.

Jason received thousands of letters congratulating him. One letter meant a great deal to him. It came from the parents of a three-year-old boy who had also been diagnosed with autism. The letter said, *Thanks for giving us hope.*

Jason McElwain, who had always been told what he couldn't do, was now a hero to millions of people. He was asked what that one night on the basketball court showed the world. Jason said, "The sky's the limit. Give it all the effort that you can. Catch a dream. And never give up."

Jason certainly didn't give up. And in this book about incredible athletes and teams, that describes unbelievable comebacks and championships, the biggest underdog among them, Jason McElwain—just 5'6"—perhaps stands the tallest of them all.